RIO MARIA

Song of the Earth

Ricardo Rezende

Translated and Edited by
Madeleine Adriance

TRÓCAIRE

ORBIS BOOKS

CIIR

The Catholic Foreign Mission Society of America (Maryknoll) recruits and trains people for overseas missionary service. Through Orbis Books, Maryknoll aims to foster the international dialogue that is essential to mission. The books published, however, reflect the opinions of their authors and are not meant to represent the official position of the society.

English translation copyright © 1994 by Orbis Books.
The Portuguese original, *Rio Maria: Canto da Terra*, copyright © 1992 by Ricardo Rezende Figueira, was published in 1992 by Editora Vozes, Rua Frei Luís 100, 25689-900 Petrópolis RJ, Brazil.
English translation published by Orbis Books, Maryknoll, New York 10545, U.S.A., CIIR (Catholic Institute for International Relations), Unit 3, Canonbury Yard, 190a New North Road, London N1 7BJ, England, and Trócaire, 169 Booterstown Avenue, Blackrock, Co. Dublin, Ireland.

Library of Congress Cataloging-in-Publication Data

Rezende, Ricardo, 1952-
   [Rio Maria. English]
   Rio Maria : song of the earth / Ricardo Rezende ;
translated and edited by Madeleine Adriance.
     p. cm.
   ISBN 0-88344-960-9
   Rezende, Ricardo, 1952- —Diaries. 2. Catholic
Church—Brazil—Rio Maria—Clergy—Diaries. 3. Rio Maria (Brazil)—
Social conditions. 4. Brazil—Social conditions. 5. Church work
with the poor—Brazil—Rio Maria—Catholic Church. 6. Rural poor—
Brazil—Rio Maria—Religious life. 7. Human ecology—Brazil—Rio
Maria—Religious aspects—Christianity. I. Adriance, Madeleine.
II. Title.
BX4705.F523A4   1994
282'.8115—dc20
[B]
                           93-49654
                            CIP

British Library Cataloguing-in-Publication Data.
A catalogue record for this book is available from the British Library.
ISBN 1 85287 126 1

In memoriam
Patrick Joseph Hanrahan
Bishop of Conceição do Araguaia 1979-1993
A great bishop, Redemptorist and Irishman,
with vigor and passion he kept alive in our diocese
the liberating flame of the gospel,
and was for us
father, brother and friend.

This book is dedicated to the representatives of the Union of Rural Workers of Rio Maria and to the relatives of the people killed in the struggle for a more humane and just country.

I would like to give special thanks to my friends André, Airton, Édna, Helena, Henri, José Batista, Juvenila, Lourdes, Lucila, Margareth, Nehida, who carry the work forward and do not bend under fear; to the pastoral teams in Rio Maria, who understand the position of the diocese and announce the Word of God in the midst of conflict; to the diocese for its support and commitment to the cause of the Kingdom; to the CPT, MEB and the Rio Maria Committees that are in solidarity with us, and visit us and support us at difficult moments and strengthen the work; and to my relatives who become frightened by the news, and to my mother who is no longer frightened and delivers me into the hands of Mary, Mother of our Lord; to my sister and brother by mutual adoption, Carla and Délcio, who opened the doors of their apartment, giving me a place to work on this book; to Betto, brother and friend, who read the text, made suggestions and extremely valuable recommendations; to Lília and Antonieta, precious friends, for their patience in reading drafts and for their very suitable suggestions.

I thank ORLATUR in São Paulo, for contributing airfare, helping with the completion of this book.

In some cases, the names of persons were changed for their protection.

Contents

Translator's Preface

Madeleine Adriance

The bus slowed its progress along the dusty road, then lurched onto a bridge and began rocking to the accompaniment of the clattering of loose boards. I tried not to think about what might happen if the bridge gave way. There were too many such crossings of streams and gullies on the road to Rio Maria for one to expend energy worrying about each of them. As the bus reached firm ground I looked out at fields of brown grass populated by grayish white cattle. A few skeletons of trees and some blackened stumps were the only signs of the rainforest that had existed here less than twenty years earlier.

This was my first trip into the southeast Amazon region of Brazil. I was on my way to meet Ricardo Rezende, a Catholic priest who was becoming known for his human rights work and his advocacy of agrarian reform. During the past twelve years nearly two hundred people, mostly poor farmers, had died in relation to land conflicts in Father Ricardo's diocese of Conceição do Araguaia in the state of Pará. Ranchers had been getting together to raise money for hiring gunmen to kill people who tried to organize the poor. There was almost complete immunity for the killers. Rarely was anyone brought to trial, and the few who were convicted were frequently allowed to escape from prison. The kind of situation that received worldwide attention with the murder of Chico Mendes was routine in southern Pará.

In Rio Maria I hoped to learn what impact the Catholic church was having on the lives of the farmers. I also wanted to know what role people in the United States could serve in this process, a role not born of guilt over our relative privilege, but emerging from a sense of human kinship. The church's advocacy for the poor appeared to have become painfully concrete in Rio Maria. A few months earlier Heloisa Andrade, a grassroots organizer and longtime friend of Father Ricardo's, had sent me a flyer announcing a large public demonstration there, aimed at putting an end to violence with impunity against peasant leaders and church people.

After crossing a few more bridges we approached a cluster of buildings that suggested a town. The bus drove down a wide street paved with hexagonal concrete slabs and came to a stop in front of a block of bars and cheap restaurants. I found the Church of Our Lady Aparecida a few blocks away. Beside the church was an area surrounded by a high wall with a wooden gate guarded by a young man wearing a tee shirt marked "Military Police." Heloisa, who had arranged my visit to Rio Maria, had told me that Father Ricardo was under the protection of the police, but that they knew I was coming. What she had not told me was that the parish house looked like a prison. The guard opened the gate for me. As I was approaching the front door of the house, a large man with a beard was coming out. I recognized him as a journalist who had been in Conceição do Araguaia the previous day, getting the story about a federal agent who had been spying on Father Ricardo. The agent's cover had been blown only a couple of days earlier, when one of the military guards had become concerned about this stranger who was spending a lot of time around the parish house. Thinking that he might present a danger to the priest, the soldier arrested him.

Inside the house I came face-to-face with a slim man with dark, wavy hair and a mustache. His eyes held a combination of warmth and keen comprehension. Father Ricardo smiled and said, "Welcome to Rio Maria."

"Thank you for letting me come," I said. "After what you've been through this week, I can't imagine why you'd let another stranger into your house."

We sat down. Father Ricardo didn't say much just then; he seemed to be waiting for me to explain myself first. I told him that I was doing research as a sociologist and that my interest in the problems of the rural poor was also related to a personal commitment to social justice. I admitted, however, that I had not yet found a practical means to put that commitment into action.

Father Ricardo went into another room and came back with articles from newspapers and magazines published in Brazil, Europe and the United States that described the situation in Rio Maria. Then he told the story in his own words, speaking with the quiet intensity of a spiritually based person who has a clear sense of the purpose of his life. He talked about the conditions that had led landless farmers to migrate to this region and, in the process, to become victims of organized violence. In the 1960s there had been a movement in northeast Brazil aimed at redistributing land among poor peasants; it was only temporarily squelched by the military coup of 1964. The generals knew that in a country in which 78 percent of the privately owned farmland is held by 10 percent of the population, it would not be possible to stifle rural unrest permanently. In the effort to protect the interests of large landowners, the military government encouraged the peasants to migrate west to the Amazon. "Land without people for people without land," was President Medici's slogan, as though the present inhabitants of the region did not count as people. The impoverished farmers who arrived in the state of Pará, however, discovered that they were not going to be given land. Large tracts of it had already been granted to wealthy individuals and companies that would install cattle ranches, destroying the rainforest in the process. Since the ranchers routinely fenced in three times as much land as they had been allotted, there was nothing left for the farmers. Whenever they would begin to work a piece of land, they would be evicted by the ranchers' hired gunmen or by the police. Many farmers were killed in the process. The Pastoral Land Commission, an agency of the Brazilian bishops that supports the efforts of poor people in organizing for agrarian reform, began to advise the farmers of their rights under federal law and to encourage them to organize unions to defend those rights. The result of those activities was the expropriation of thousands of acres by the government for redistribution. The ranchers retaliated with even more violence against the farmers, as well as against union leaders and staff members of the Pastoral Land Commission.

During the most turbulent years, from 1978 to 1988, Ricardo Rezende was working for this commission, first as a layman, later as a priest. In addition to losing several of his friends to assassins' bullets, he was repeatedly the target of death threats and of actual attempts on his life.

In 1988 Father Ricardo went to live in Rio Maria. Since the diocese of Conceição do Araguaia was short of priests, he decided that it was time that he did parish work. Also, he believed that all the attention that journalists were giving personally to him was becoming counterproductive for the Pastoral Land Commission. He chose Rio Maria because it was out of the spotlight. There were no telephones there at the time, and there was much less violence than in other towns in the region. Within fifteen months of his arrival, however, phone lines were installed and five people associated with the land movement were killed. There was also an automobile accident that nearly took his life and that many people believed was not really accidental.

Around the time of the demonstration in March 1991 Father Ricardo got together with several people who wanted to stop the violence. They decided to organize a network of Rio Maria Committees in several cities in the center-south of the country—Rio de Janeiro, São Paulo, Juiz de Fora—as well as in Pará. By the time that I met Father Ricardo these committees had spread to Europe, and he told me that one had recently begun in London. I asked him, "If there were to be a Rio Maria Committee in the United States, what would be its function?" He focused those compelling eyes on me, smiled and asked, "Do you have a fax machine?"

It was my turn to smile. The man who came to Rio Maria to get away from phones was now at the center of an electronic network.

On my return home I started the U.S. branch of the Rio Maria Committee, which organizes letter-writing campaigns to encourage Brazilian government officials to take action against the violence in the southeast Amazon. We have already seen results. There have been dates set for murder trials that were stalled for many years. Federal Police protection has been maintained for union leaders whose lives were threatened. The outcome of all this is that, during the past two years, there has been a measurable decrease in violence in the region around Rio Maria.

Our efforts in the United States got a boost in 1992 with the visit of Father Ricardo. He has a special effect on people, with his way of being fully present with each one he meets. The personal problems of individuals seem to be of as much concern to him as broader social issues. During his public talks in the Boston area, for which I served as interpreter, I was struck by the way that his warmth transcended the language barrier. "I was so moved," someone later told me. "He's such a nice guy," said another person, "not just a social crusader." "Make sure he knows," said a priest who had invited Father Ricardo to speak at his church, "that I felt really privileged to have him here, to concelebrate mass with him."

There is so much to say about Father Ricardo and about Rio Maria, but it is best to let him tell the story himself. It was a fortunate coincidence that when he became pastor of Our Lady Aparecida, he decided to start keeping a journal. Since he had chosen that parish because it seemed quiet, it is likely that he had no idea that included in his random notes would be a record of events that would be of interest to people all over Brazil, as well as in the United States and Britain. Neither did he have any idea that those events would lead to further threats on his life, to travel to Europe and North America and to his receiving the Chico Mendes Award from a group of Brazilian human rights groups and the Silver Medal from Anti-Slavery International. In the midst of his recording of his everyday experiences in a rural town — from celebrating mass to having to use an outhouse infested by bees — there also appeared accounts of the events leading up to assassinations that have focused international attention on Rio Maria.

It has been my privilege to translate this journal. What appears on these pages is not an exact rendering of the volume published in Portuguese. In writing for an English-speaking audience, I have edited and in some places rewritten this account, but with Father Ricardo's permission and with a concern to preserve the essential message of a man who is fearless in the face of danger because of his serene conviction that his life is in God's hands and that he is doing what he was called to do.

Father Ricardo's experience of calling may have been unusual in the way that it came through the local church community. It was at the urging of lay people in the diocese of Conceição do Araguaia that he, as a young staff member of the Pastoral Land Commission, approached Bishop Joseph Hanrahan to ask to be considered for ordination. A priest in the south of Pará, however, cannot confine himself to conducting religious rituals while shutting his eyes to the suffering of the people. So Father Ricardo's spiritual commitment has pushed him into the midst of the land struggle, and his personal charisma has pushed him, much to his chagrin, back into the media spotlight. He is always concerned that the attention of journalists may be focused more on him than on the hundreds of impoverished farmers being killed. Let us hope that the publication of his journal, while related to his growing fame, will help to call attention, as is his wish, to the suffering of the people of the southeast Amazon and to the positive results of international mobilization in support of their efforts to build a just society.

Five people provided invaluable assistance in producing the English-language version of this book. I am grateful to Tanya Gardiner-Scott for critical comments on translations of the poetry, to Dalmir da Silva for help with slang and regional expressions, to Paula Ford for enthusiastic feedback on early drafts of some passages and to Joanna Berkman and Father Joe Rozansky for reading the entire manuscript against a deadline and offering very helpful suggestions. I am especially grateful to Joanna for giving me advice and encouragement throughout this whole project.

Dramatis Personae

(listed alphabetically by first name)

Ademir Andrade—former federal senator of the Socialist Party, representing the state of Pará

Father Aristide Camió—a French missionary priest who was imprisoned for two years under the military regime

Adilson Laranjeira—former mayor of Rio Maria, involved in planning the murder of João Canuto

Airton—a seminarian on the pastoral team in Rio Maria

Aninha (Ana de Souza Pinto)—staff member of the Pastoral Land Commission in Conceição do Araguaia

Antônio Vieira—president of the Teachers' Union of Rio Maria

Aprígio Menezes Soares—a gunman who works at the Suaçuí Ranch

Batista—See José Batista

Braguinha (Geraldo de Oliveira Braga)—owner of the Suaçuí Ranch

Brás Antônio de Oliveira—former officer of the Union of Rural Workers, a cowhand who became a mechanic

Carlos Cabral—current president of the Union of Rural Workers of Rio Maria, married to Luzia, daughter of João Canuto

Expedito Ribeiro de Souza—poet and union president in Rio Maria

Dona Francisca—a woman from the Vila Nova neighborhood who is active in the church

Dona Geraldina—widow of João Canuto

Gringo (Raimundo Ferreira Lima)—a union activist killed on May 29, 1980

Guaracy Baschiglia—an agronomist who works for the Pastoral Land Commission in Conceição do Araguaia

Father Henri des Roziers—a French Dominican and attorney who worked for many years for the Pastoral Land Commission and currently works in Rio Maria

Father Hilário Lopes—parish priest in Xinguara until 1992

Heloisa Andrade—worked for many years in the church's Basic Education Movement in Conceição do Araguaia

Jerônimo Treccani—director of Pastoral Land Commission in Pará

Jesuino Pereira de Souza—farmer, organizer of base communities, former officer of the Union of Rural Workers

João Canuto—president of Union of Rural Workers of Rio Maria, assassinated on December 18, 1985

João Martins—a farmer who is active in the church and who was one of the key witnesses in the murder of João Canuto

Dom José (Bishop Joseph Hanrahan)—bishop of Conceição do Araguaia 1979–93

José Batista—a seminarian on the pastoral team in Rio Maria

José Canuto—son of João Canuto

José Ricardo—brother of Carlos Cabral

Jurandir—gunman involved in the murder of João Canuto, brother-in-law of João Martins

Sister Lourdes Follman—religious of the congregation of the Daughters of Divine Love who works in Rio Maria

Lula (Luís Inácio Lula da Silva)—union activist and presidential candidate from the Workers' Party (PT)

Luzia Canuto—one of the few women in Rio Maria who has suffered death threats, daughter of João Canuto, married to Carlos Cabral

Marciel Canuto—youngest son of João Canuto

Dona Maria—parish housekeeper

Memélia Moreira—a journalist who works in Brasília

Miriam Furtado de Mendonça—works in the church's Basic Education Movement in Conceição do Araguaia

Sister Nehida—religious of the congregation of the Daughters of Divine Love who worked in Rio Maria until 1993

Neném Simão—rancher involved in the murder of João Canuto

Neto (Manoel Barbosa Milhomem)—a nineteen-year-old gunman

Nivaldo Vieira de Nascimento—staff member of the Pastoral Land Commission in Conceição do Araguaia

Orlando Canuto—son of João Canuto

Paulo Canuto—son of João Canuto

Paulo Fonteles—attorney who defended the rural workers, assassinated on June 11, 1987

Father Pedro das Neves—parish priest in Xinguara until 1993

Pedro Vieira—former police chief in Rio Maria

Roberto Neto da Silva—president of the Communist Party in Rio Maria and active member of the Union of Rural Workers

Sebastião Vieira—City Councilor of the Socialist Party, brother of schoolteacher Antônio Vieira

Terms and Abbreviations

base communities — small groups of lay people who gather to study the Bible and to discuss its relevance to their lives

CONTAG — national federation of unions of rural workers

CPT — Pastoral Land Commission, agency of the Brazilian Bishops

CNBB — National Conference of the Brazilian Bishops

CUT — national labor federation

Dona — term of respect preceding the first name of an older woman

Dom — term of respect preceding the first name of a bishop

IBAMA — government agency charged with the protection of the Amazon

MEB — Basic Education Movement — a church-related organization that provides instruction in literacy and political education

PC do B — Communist Party of Brazil, distinct from the now-defunct, Soviet-oriented Brazilian Communist Party

PSB — Brazilian Socialist Party

PT — Workers' Party

posseiro — a person who, under Brazilian law, gains the right to a piece of public land by farming it for a year and a day

SUDAM — federal agency which gave financial incentives to companies and individuals to install cattle ranches in the Amazon

Seu — term of respect preceding the first name of an older man

UDR — national organization of ranchers and large landowners

Introduction

Gary MacEoin

Few people know Northern Brazil as profoundly and lovingly as theologian José Comblin. As I read, fascinated, Father Ricardo Rezende Figueira's record of his immersion as a pastor in a typical area of Amazonia, I constantly recalled a thought once formulated by Comblin. "The experience of God found in the new Christian communities [of this and other parts] of Latin America can properly be called experience of the Holy Spirit."

Joachim di Fiore, a twelfth-century Italian monk, was the first known utopian. He interpreted the human experience as an ongoing process that would reach its culmination and perfection within human history, not in some posthistorical eschaton. Starting from the Trinitarian doctrine that is central to all Christian belief, he divided the history of salvation into three phases. The first, linked to God the Father, ran from Adam to Jesus. The second, linked to God the Son, still continued. It would, however, soon yield to the era of God the Spirit, an era of justice more perfect than all that had gone before. It certainly demands an immense leap of faith to interpret the story Father Ricardo tells as the introduction to an era of justice. Yet for me it is possible to make sense of the unequal struggle of his dispossessed and voiceless friends only if we interpret it dialectically as the opening of the apocalyptic struggle that we know by faith will end in the destruction of the near-omnipotent Beast.

Father Ricardo has strengthened my conviction that we have to give a more mystical and positive interpretation to the oft-quoted statement of Jesus that the poor we shall always have with us. Let us read it in the context of that other promise of Jesus that the poor shall inherit the earth. Always with us, indeed. But not as poor. Instead, as survivors, the only survivors, survivors finally in possession of their abundant heritage.

The reality of life in Brazil (as generally in Latin America) has never been of major interest to most people in the United States, and today it has become even more marginal to the concerns of the electronic and printed media than during the short-lived popularity of the Alliance for Progress in the 1960s. The U.S. government has proclaimed the era of democracy, ignoring the reality that the most one can have is a facade and a mockery of democracy where the majority of citizens are hungry, powerless and illiterate. The State Department proclaims progress in human rights and in protection of the ecology of the Amazonian forests that are critical to the survival of the planet.

Father Ricardo's day-by-day and killing-by-killing account of life and death in his vast parish of Rio Maria, diocese of Conceição, state of Pará, in Brazil's southeast Amazon, explodes that cynical misrepresentation. Here only a few wealthy ranchers (and their private armies of assassins), the military, the police, the judges and the mayors have rights. Even the peasant squatters, who in theory are protected by law, have no redress when a rancher destroys their shacks and plows under the crops grown on soil made fertile by years of sweat and calloused hands.

Laws protecting the ecology are on the statute books. They are enforced against the peasants whose burnings are relatively trivial. Corporate enterprises burn thousands of acres with impunity.

Violent death is omnipresent. The most frequent targets are union organizers and social workers who challenge the system, including priests and other church workers. But it can happen almost casually. An entry in Father Ricardo's diary for May 1989 reads: "One of these ranchers hired a peon who took a fancy to the manager's wife. So he authorized the manager to put an end to the peon. The manager beat him to death, threw him into a 200-liter drum, boiled him and fed him to the pigs." This is typical of the way ranchers treat their workers. Rape of women is almost routine, and it is not uncommon to kill a worker who has completed a major land-clearance assignment rather than pay him.

The social chaos is well communicated by political scientist Ricardo Kotscho in his Introduction to the original Portuguese version of the diary published in Brazil in 1992. "Death has been banalized. People are no longer killed only in disputes over money or over land ownership. They kill on a whim, for any reason or none. Impunity is guaranteed. But how have we reached this state of affairs? When in the middle of the decade [of the 1980s] the military were invited by the huge crowds who took possession of the streets in the Campaign of Rights to return to their barracks, we thought that Brazil was entering a new phase, putting an end to official terrorism and opening the way to becoming a minimally civilized nation. What happened was the exact opposite. Ricardo Rezende's diary fixes for us the exact moment when this lurch backward occurred: in 1985, with the civilian government of [President] Sarney firmly in place, the 'security businesses' came to life, namely the paramilitary forces that institutionalized terror and death as control mechanisms."

As long as this state of lawlessness remains the substance of Brazil's new order, the United States can take no accolade for whatever part it played in papering over the military misrule with the veneer of what the State Department euphemistically calls incipient democracy.

Father Ricardo's diary was not composed with an international readership in mind. Indeed, many elements in the Portuguese original would make little sense to the average U.S. reader. I can only marvel at Madeleine Adriance's admirable job of editing and annotating. Once I picked it up, I could not put it down.

There is a tremendous urgency about Father Ricardo's message. We have learned a lot about the barbarities of Brazil's military regime in the 1960s and 1970s, thanks to the efforts of courageous Brazilian religious leaders, Catholic and Protestant, who documented the obscenities of the torture chambers in *Brazil, Never Again!* But make no mistake. Even if the military have gone back to their barracks, they have not yielded the ultimate power to the civilian regimes that survive at their toleration. Their mentality is unchanged. They believe that they are justified in using any and every means to achieve their objectives. They remain committed to defend the rich against the poor. The fight for human rights has not yet been won. We have a long way to go before we can declare: *Brazil, Never Again! Guatemala, Never Again! Haiti, Never Again! Anywhere, Never Again!*

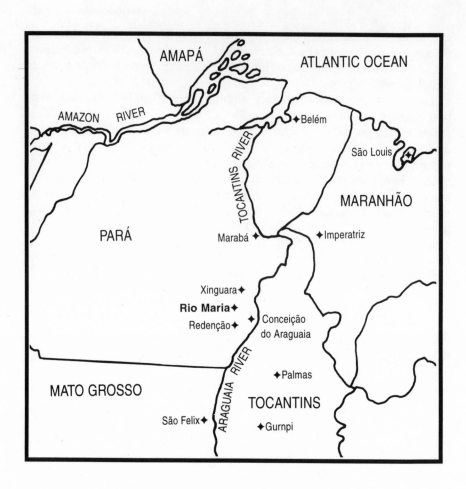

1.

1980 to 1988

Father Ricardo reminisces about his ordination day, then moves on to October 1988 when he is leaving the Pastoral Land Commission to become pastor in Rio Maria. This leads him to think about the union leader João Canuto, who used to live there. After telling the story of João, Father Ricardo introduces the contemporary situation. He tells us about some of the people in Rio Maria, including the poet and union president Expedito Ribeiro de Souza, three missionary sisters from the far south of Brazil and other members of the Canuto family. He also relates stories that give a sense of the everyday level of violence.

Rower, let the boat go where it will,
Let these waters carry us yonder.
Yet they always bring us back,
For the Araguaia releases no one.

July, 1980. Conceição do Araguaia, Pará. The dry season heat is intense. The waters of the Araguaia River have receded, leaving dots of sandy islands that attract tourists. Bathers stretch out lazily on the sands and children run through the water, while municipal workers gather up bottles, cans and papers. Pequi trees display an abundance of flowers and the branches of cashew trees are sagging with fruit. The cathedral of Conceição is full. Friends from the countryside, from the city and from more distant places are singing "Araguaia, My Araguaia."

The rite of ordination begins. Between white columns we walk through the church that has been decorated with care and devotion. The wall of wood separating the sacristy from the altar is adorned with green branches and flowers. There is a huge banner which reads "JUSTICE WILL BE LIKE A GARMENT THAT HE PUTS ON." On the left side there is a picture of Our Lady of the Immaculate Conception and an enlarged black and white photograph of Gringo.[1]

After the penitential rite, the people sing:

> The life that we live
> Is full of division,
> But that's not what God wants
> That's not what God wants.

The first reading is from the book of Isaiah: "This is my servant, for whom I care, the one whom I chose and whom I love . . . He shall do justice to the poor of the land." We then listen to the Second Letter of Saint Paul to Timothy: "Take your share of suffering for the gospel . . . Spread the Word of God, whether convenient or not." We also hear from Matthew 5: "You are the salt of people's lives. If salt loses its flavor how can we restore it? . . . No one lights a lamp to hide it under a basket, but to place it on a stand where it gives light to all in the house."

I stretch out face down on the cool floor of the church during the recitation of the litany prepared by Dom Pedro Casaldáliga, Bishop of São Félix do Araguaia.

> Indians, peons, cow hands and gold prospectors, fathers and mothers of families, young people and children who died in the peace of the Lord in these hinterlands and forests;
>   João Bosco, Rodolfo, Simão Bororo, Raimundo, Gringo, Archbishop Romero, Santo Dias and all the martyrs of the cause of the people, who learned how to face up to injustice and to love their brothers and sisters even unto death.

Once anointed and ordained, I am presented to the people and to my parents as a priest. My father cries, while my mother looks serene. I feel moved at the sight of friends with tears on their faces.

The offertory procession begins with symbols of the base communities[2] that live a religious and social commitment. João Canuto brings a papaya, Manoel Gago a hoe, Belchior an ax, Sinhozinho a screwdriver — instruments of work and fruits of the land. Others bring the bible, a roofing tile, a T-square, a fisherman's oar, a book, a piece of chalk, an oil lamp, bread and wine. Cantídio, an Indian of the Tapirapé tribe, who came in the name of the Prelacy of São Félix do Araguaia, is carrying a gourd rattle and a

1. Raimundo Ferreira Lima, killed on May 29, 1980. He was a candidate for president of the Union of Rural Workers of Conceição do Araguaia.

2. Base communities are small groups of lay people who gather to study the Bible and to discuss its relevance to their lives. Since most members of base communities in Brazil are poor, this discussion often leads to social or political action — tr.

wooden stool that has ritual significance. During the procession Expedito, a black poet from Minas Gerais, recites a poem written for the occasion.

> God, Lord All-powerful,
> Father of fathers, God of Love,
> Cast your eyes on our gifts.
> Omnipotent Lord,
> As we are offering
> The labor of farmers.
> We also are offering
> In total sincerity
> The work of this youth
> Who now is a priest
> So that he may be happy
> Doing your will.

To the left of the altar I see Paulo Fonteles,[3] the lawyer, with goatee and glasses, prematurely bald. He is smirking at me. In the middle of the church is Gabriel Pimenta,[4] a friend from my hometown who recently finished law school.

Gringo seems to be giving us a hard look through his thick-framed glasses. His picture is as commanding as a shout within the church, a cry that summons us. Singing along with the congregation is Oneide, his widow.

Later, after I've been hugged by everyone and am still standing inside the church, Benícia tells me, "We're throwing a party for you tonight."

She has pulled down the inside walls of her house to make room for dancing. My parents, Roberto, Dona[5] Maria Pereira, Heloisa and many other special friends are all there, shuffling their feet. Dona Maria Pimenta leaves her partner and drags me into the dance. Another friend smiles and comments:

"Ordained this morning by the bishop. Now by the people as well."

Saturday, October 29, 1988. Conceição do Araguaia. I've worked for eleven and a half years for the Pastoral Land Commission. We set up an office for advising rural workers of their rights. Now I'm going to be pastor of Rio Maria, 180 kilometers from here. I feel pain in this separation. One falls in love with one's friends, with one's work. One grows accustomed to the Araguaia River, so beautiful in its curves, in its color. One gets used to the angles of the backyard, the trees, the pictures on the walls, the books

3. Paulo Fonteles was hired by the Pastoral Land Commission to give legal help to the rural workers of the diocese of Conceiço do Araguaia. He was assassinated on June 11, 1987.

4. Gabriel Pimenta was killed in July 1982, in Marabá, Pará.

5. "Dona" is the term of respect preceding the given name of an older woman—tr.

on the shelves. This bookcase makes me think of João Canuto, a long-time friend I'll never see again.

In December 1979, when Doza, Heloísa and I moved into this house, there was no place for books. João and another peasant farmer were passing through the city. As usual they stayed with us. I asked them to build us the bookcase.

Now I'm packing my suitcases, getting ready to move to the town where João lived. I'm remembering this thin man, 51 years old, with huge glasses, a narrow mustache, and the gentle voice of someone who never got angry and was never in a rush. The struggle? "It's for a whole lifetime."

He was a leader of the base community in Vila Nova, a poor neighborhood in Rio Maria, where he discovered the need for grassroots organization. Encouraged by those of us who worked in the Pastoral Land Commission, he became a candidate for the directorate of the Union of Rural Workers. In 1982, when Rio Maria became a separate municipal district, he ran for mayor.

A poor farmer who had been thrown off the land, João Canuto ran his campaign without a car and without money. Early in the morning he would leave his hut, which had a thatched roof, a dirt floor and a flimsy privy in the backyard, and would go out by bicycle with Expedito, the poet, to win the hearts of the people. The two of them would ride, looking like unfurled flags, along dusty roads and rough trails through the woods, over hills and through streets of the town, bringing hope to the suffering. João would communicate a certainty of better times in his unhurried, patient conversations, while Expedito would spontaneously compose beautiful verses. Later the poor farmers all said that he won the election in terms of votes, but lost because of fraud. Adilson Laranjeira became mayor of Rio Maria.

In 1983 João Canuto participated in the creation of the new Union of Rural Workers of Rio Maria and became its first president. The death threats that he had been receiving intensified over the next couple of years. He complained to the local police and to authorities in Belém.

At eleven thirty on the morning of December 18, 1985, two strangers walked into a bar in the red light district located between the center of Rio Maria and João Canuto's neighborhood of Vila Nova. One was a tall, thin man with dark hair and light skin, wearing a blue cap, jeans and a striped shirt. The other was short, dark and dressed in beige slacks and a white shirt. They ordered beer. One man leaned against the end of the bar, while the other stood further down, facing the street. He kept going to the door and looking outside. Finally the bar maid, Maria de Lourdes Silva, asked:

"You guys are uneasy. Waiting for someone?"

After saying that they were waiting for their company car, they paid for the beers and left. Maria de Lourdes watched them walk across the road to the old cemetery. They sat down for a few minutes, then came back to the bar.

"Do you have poor man's whiskey?"

Maria de Lourdes reached for the liter of cane liquor and served them. After downing four shots they went out to the street and sat down in front of the shack of Luzia Tavares da Silva, an illiterate woman of fifty well-lived years. Luzia was taking a nap when she was awakened by a creaking sound. She got up, opened the door and saw the two strangers leaning against her outside wall and talking in whispers. Luzia quickly shut the door.

After about thirty minutes, the taller man went back into the bar and asked for a match. Before Maria de Lourdes could give him one, the shorter man called him from outside and the two of them ran off in the direction of the cemetery. Maria de Lourdes hurried to the doorway. She saw João Canuto coming down the street. When he was about to pass the taller of the two men, the stranger took out a pistol and, at point-blank range, pulled the trigger. Maria de Lourdes heard three loud claps. She saw João fall. The shorter man knelt and fired several more shots into him.

Today João Canuto becomes more present not only in the boards of this bookcase, but all over this house. Eight years ago he attended my ordination along with Belchior Martins, Paulo Fonteles, Gabriel Pimenta, Manoel Gago and Sinhozinho. Today these six friends can celebrate face-to-face with God. All of them were assassinated.

Monday, October 31. Yesterday Bishop Joseph Hanrahan installed me as pastor in Rio Maria. The people received me with affection. Rio Maria is a tiny city between Redenção and Xinguara. There are around fifteen thousand inhabitants in town and about the same number in the countryside. The population is composed of landless farmers, squatters, gold prospectors, businessmen, landowners, public employees and lumber-yard workers. People come from all parts of this country, driven by necessity and looking for a means to survive and raise their children, but often finding violence and death. I had previously visited this parish in the course of my work with the Pastoral Land Commission. I had followed the eviction from the Marajoara Ranch and the struggle of the *posseiros*[6] on the Canaan Ranch. Those were difficult times. Now the town is living through a period of relative calm.

The sisters who work here are Daughters of Divine Love, who are from the state of Rio Grande do Sul. Sister Lucila, a retired nurse, is thin with blond hair turning white. Sister Nehida is tall and very fair-skinned, with short, black hair. Since she likes to walk fast, one of the parishioners has nicknamed her "Speedy." Sister Lourdes is a hard-working woman in her

---

6. According to Brazilian law, a person who farms a piece of unused land for a year and a day has the right to remain on it, although usually without being given written title. Such a person is called a *posseiro*. Most of the land conflicts in the region around Rio Maria are between *posseiros* and large ranchers — tr.

early forties with light blond hair. During her years in Pará her Gaucho-German[7] accent has been fading.

These sisters are of the same congregation as Sister Adelaide Molinari, who was killed in Curionópolis in 1985. She had been talking with a union leader, when a hired gunman took aim for him. The bullet entered his back, passed through his shoulder and hit the sister in the neck. The unionist survived. Sister Adelaide fell and died in a pool of blood.

Tuesday, November 1. Dona Oneide is so thin that her bones are visible. She doesn't come to church often, but today she had something to tell me.

"The ranchers have decided to kill you."

"Where did you hear this?"

"In the school while I was cleaning."

"Who said it?"

"I heard Antônio the teacher saying it." She paused. "You know that it is dangerous to talk about these things. They could do away with me."

I thanked her. She left.

Wednesday, November 2. All Souls' Day. I celebrated mass in the two cemeteries. The old one, full of undergrowth, has been abandoned by the mayor's office. They want people to transfer their dead to the new cemetery, but the funeral service is charging 250,000 cruzeiros (US $481[8]).

Thursday, November 3. A young couple was waiting to see me. The man introduced himself as Augusto, brother of Carlos Cabral,[9] and presented his wife and their baby. They are living temporarily with Carlos and his wife Luzia.

"I used to live near the gunman Porfírio," Augusto explained. "One day he came to my house and said, 'A guy in the bar over there is going around saying that he's hiring two men to kill me. Come with me and we'll take care of him. You're my friend, right?' I answered, 'Friend for that kind of thing I'm not.' "

Porfírio went to the bar, drank and got into a conversation with the guy he believed was planning to kill him. Augusto took advantage of his absence to say to his pregnant wife, "Pretend you're going into labor. Groan a lot. Get two neighbors to help you. You have to keep me from going with him." The gunman came back with a dark, thin young man who said he was a gold prospector.

---

7. "Gaucho" is the name given in Brazil to natives of the state of Rio Grande do Sul, where there is a large number of people of German descent — tr.

8. The value of Brazilian currency is constantly changing. Wherever there is a reference to money, the comparable value in dollars shown in parentheses will be that which the author calculated at that particular time — tr.

9. Carlos Cabral is married to João Canuto's daughter Luzia — tr.

Porfírio insisted that Augusto go with them. At that point the wife started groaning.

The two neighbors appeared and Augusto begged off.

Porfírio took the prospector to a nearby house, shot him five times and bashed his head with the pistol. Later he went back to Augusto's home and spoke to him in a menacing tone.

"From this day on you are my enemy. If you tell anyone what I've done I'll kill you."

Fearing for his life, Augusto moved in with Carlos.

He also told me about the time that his brother stopped by the house of a farmer named Baiano and found his corpse. Baiano was a sharecropper working for a gunman named Zezinho on land owned by a rancher from Redenção. Zezinho had an agreement with the rancher to plant and harvest the land, then convert it to pasture. When he saw Baiano's good crop, he decided not to share the harvest. He hired two men who killed the peasant and raped his wife and his ten-year-old daughter.

Carlos reported the crime to Sergeant Pedrosa, who arrested the gunmen. Then Carlos went to see the judge in Conceição do Araguaia, but when he got back, he found that not only were the gunmen free, but also that Zezinho was threatening him. Zezinho ended up being killed a few days later by an unknown man.

After Augusto and his wife left I went to talk with the schoolteacher, Antônio Vieira, about what Dona Oneide had said. There had been a misunderstanding. He had mentioned that someone could decide to kill me, but Oneide thought it was already decided.

Friday, November 4. After celebrating an early mass with the sisters, I went with Dona Francisca and Sister Lourdes to visit people in the countryside. Dona Francisca was asking her friends for contributions of food for a feast that she had helped organize to raise money for a chapel in Vila Nova. She informed me that she was expecting me to be there.

This evening Expedito, the poet who is president of the union and a candidate for mayor, was here for dinner. He talked about local land problems, mentioning that, after the government expropriated some ranches in Rio Maria, the small farmers did not get titles to the land, despite the efforts of the union and the Pastoral Land Commission. They had even gone to Brasília, but got nowhere with the federal government.

"It's a scandal," he complained. "They expropriate land only after conflict and death. Nothing happens without conflict."

In addition to the problem of titles, the farmers were suffering because of the lack of schools, roads, medical care and decent prices for their products.

After we finished eating, I remembered Dona Francisca's insistence that I show up at the feast. Since I didn't know the exact location, I asked

Expedito to come with me. On the way I began to have doubts about what we were doing.

"People are going to talk about the priest hanging out with the Communist candidate," I said to Expedito. "And not just hanging out, but even going with him to the feast for the chapel."

We drove through the red light district, with its women and young girls on display, then passed by the old cemetery. At the high point of Vila Nova, between simple houses and shacks, we saw the sound truck. The feast looked like a rally for the Socialist Party, with political posters everywhere. The candidates for town council and for mayor were present. They looked at me in surprise, perhaps annoyed because I was arriving with the candidate of another party.[10] I decided not to stay long.

We stopped by the Canuto home and got a warm welcome from João's widow, Dona Geraldina, a small, thin woman with premature wrinkles. As I looked around the room, filled with sons, daughters-in-law and grandchildren, I got to thinking how the old and the new coexist. People were talking about socialism. Yet hanging above the door was the traditional picture of Jesus with his gentle gaze and the rays of light around his heart.

---

10. Expedito was the mayoral candidate for the PC do B, the Communist Party of Brazil, which is distinct from the Soviet-linked Brazilian Communist Party (which no longer exists), as well as from the Workers' Party (PT) and the Socialist Party (PSB)— tr.

2.

January 14 to January 28, 1989

After a two-month hospitalization following a suspicious acci-
dent, Father Ricardo returns to Rio Maria and begins to
acquire closer knowledge of the situation there. A visit to a
ranch shows the strain that already exists in his relationship to
large landowners. A positive element that appears is world-
wide solidarity, as evidenced in dozens of letters from mem-
bers of Amnesty International.

Saturday, January 14. I was in a collision on November 8 in Belém, on my way to speak at the law school. A truck hit the car in which I was riding with three students. Two of them received minor injuries. I ended up with a fractured skull and went into a coma. I'm alive after two operations, and I'm getting ready for the third one, which will be done in Minas Gerais. The UDR[1] will have to put up with me a little longer, God willing. Some newspapers that came out after the collision suggested that it was no accident.

I arrived in Rio Maria yesterday, passing through Conceição do Araguaia and hitching a ride with Guaracy[2] as far as Redenção. After I put my suitcase in my room I learned about two burglaries in parish houses, one in Xinguara, the other in Rio Maria. In the first the thieves took a sound system, bed linens and towels. In my house they only took an electric iron.

Father Hilário Lopes came over from Xinguara. He brought two Franciscan seminarians, who are doing part of their training with us, and Maria Rocha, widow of Atenor Moreira ("Tena"). Tena had asked me to be godfather to their baby; he was killed while I was in the hospital. Maria Rocha spoke with deep sadness about her husband, who was attacked by

1. UDR, the Democratic Rural Union, is the national interest group of ranchers and large landowners—tr.

2. Guaracy Baschiglia, a young agronomist who works for the Pastoral Land Commission in Conceição do Araguaia—tr.

four men because of his leadership in land issues. He was taken to the São Francisco Hospital in Rio Maria, where he died on Christmas Day.

Monday, January 16. Expedito visited me this afternoon. He said that six bodies were found in the area of Bambuzal, on the road to Floresta.

"The Union sent reports about this to the mayor and the police chief, but didn't get an answer. People are afraid to walk down that road. The smell of the bodies is awful."

Wednesday, January 18. I received a message to call my friend Memélia Moreira, a journalist, and immediately went to the telephone station. Several people were waiting for booths. Although the company collected money some years ago to install phones in people's homes, they still have not done so.

When I reached Memélia, she told me that the newspaper, *OGlobo*, published an article about death threats, and that there was a picture of me. Then she laughed and said that it came out well, in spite of my bald head. My head had been shaven because of the surgery after the accident in Belém.

Friday, January 20. A lot of letters from France have been coming through the parish post office box for Dona Geraldina, widow of João Canuto. Batista, the seminarian who is working in this parish, took the mail to her home. She had received others and confessed to me that she could not understand them.

"They are always in a foreign language," she lamented.

I translated the letters for her. Marciel, her youngest son, was picking up the empty envelopes. The other sons, José, Paulo and Orlando, listened in silence. The letters had been written at the encouragement of Amnesty International, and expressed solidarity and affection. The police chief has also received letters asking about the inquest regarding Canuto's murder.

Yesterday I called Conceição do Araguaia and talked with a young German volunteer who is working for the CPT (Pastoral Land Commission). He said that the mayor of Conceição had been asking for information about farmers killed over land disputes, because he, too, had received letters from Amnesty International.

Later that day Dona Maria[3] went to the post office and picked up thirty-three more letters from France for Dona Geraldina.

9 P.M. A young man with a shoulder bag came to the front door. I could not see him clearly in the weak light, and felt uncertain about coming any closer. He sat outside, on the edge of the well, with his face still in the shadows. He said that he had gone to the sisters' house looking for a place to spend the night and they sent him to me. He was from Maranhão and

3. Dona Maria is the parish housekeeper — tr.

had been a victim of forced labor on the Belauto Ranch.

"Things are rough there. They beat the workers and withhold wages. Workers can leave only by running away."

He said that he had malaria. He paused and passed his hands over his eyes, looking like he was crying. He asked for food and a place to hang his hammock. After several attempts on my life, I was feeling hesitant about letting a stranger sleep here.

I asked his name. Adão Santana Silva. He is 21 years old and single. We went looking for a place for him to stay. Beside the bus station there is a small boarding house and a restaurant. I gave him money for accommodations and food and arranged to meet him tomorrow.

Saturday, January 21. Early in the morning Adão came to the parish house. While he spoke I wrote notes.

"A labor contractor named Pedro hired me in November," he said. "He came to my town, offering advance money for those of us who wanted to come. I got 4,000 cruzeiros (US $4.73), but there were workers who got as much as 10,000. The following day they drove about forty of us on a truck. We reached the Belauto Ranch on November 5. We were divided into teams. Pedro had four gunmen. The contract was for clearing 170 acres of forest for pasture. They promised that they would pay 10,000 cruzeiros per acre and that they would also give us food. Some of the men did not believe them and ran away. I was sick from the beginning and asked to leave during the first month. The contractor said I could not, and he gave me some pills. The one who really helped me was a fellow worker, old João. He prepared some remedies and gave me garlic to eat. With that help I was able to continue. At the end of the contract there were only six of us left, including a woman, Dona Raimunda." Adão stopped to take a sip of the coffee that Dona Maria had brought us. "One day the gunmen caught two workers who were trying to escape. They tied them to a steam shovel, beat them, then sent them back to work. Three days later they ran away again. On January 14 we told the contractor that the work was done and that we were going to leave. He said that he was going to give us another fifteen hundred acres. We got scared. On January 17 we decided to escape. We followed the trail at night, and at the first light of dawn went into the woods. We walked eighty kilometers without stopping, from the beginning of night until sunrise. We went to São Félix do Xingu. Old João and Dona Raimunda stayed there. The others decided to become gold prospectors. I wanted to go home, but first we told our story to the local police. Someone told us that they wouldn't do anything because the rancher is rich. I invited my companions to go to the Military Police in Marabá, but they didn't want to. They said that we would be marked and persecuted."

"Could you make a report through the Union of Rural Workers?" I asked.

"I'm afraid to do it by myself, because Pedro knows where I live. If the whole group had wanted to make a report, I would have done it."

I gave him money to continue his trip home.

Carlos Cabral, João Canuto's son-in-law, came over to show me a letter written last November by the union to the mayor, reporting the deaths on the road to Floresta.

"The gunman Porfírio," said Carlos, "was killed in a mining camp. Another one who probably won't live long is his horrible nephew, Neto. Although he's still a teenager, he is believed to have been involved in the murder of a farmer last year at Canaan. On the day when Porfírio died, Neto was with a cousin in the doorway of the Maringá dance hall. The cousin stuck out his leg to trip a peon. When the peon saw who the boys were, he got scared and begged forgiveness. Neto, laughing, said to his cousin, 'No, we don't forgive,' and shot the man in the mouth."

Carlos urged me not to stay in the parish house alone. "Just before your accident in Belém, I heard a lot of talk around the bus station that you were going to die, which was what I heard just before my father-in-law was killed."

Six young people came over to study the Gospel of Mark with Batista, Sister Lourdes and me. We studied the preaching of John the Baptist, the baptism of Jesus and the first miracles. The story of the expulsion of the demons reminded someone of Pentecostal ministers.

"They claim that they work miracles and expel demons. One minister came to town with a powerful sound system. He called the people to the square. When they brought a sick man, he cried out for Satan to leave the suffering one. Then he collected a lot of money."

We talked about the presence of the devil among us and about his works: hunger, misery, exploitation, injustice and violence. We discussed how to put an end to this force of evil.

Wednesday, January 25. Dona Maria brought coffee, then sat down in my office, draped the dish towel over her shoulder and wiped the sweat off her face.

"Bus trips are so expensive and so hard. The buses delay, break down or turn around. I travel with a tight heart. Last May I was coming from Redenção when, at the Salobro bridge, we saw people grouped together. The driver stepped on the brakes and cried out in surprise. I looked out and saw two bodies beside the bridge. Ave Maria! We got off to get a better look. The dead men were young, wearing shorts, and covered with bruises. I went down into the gully. Holy Virgin! Two more bodies! No one ever found out who those boys were. They could have been workers who fled from a ranch. They could have been gold prospectors. Only God can make sense of this world."

Saturday, January 28. Yesterday there was a free political program for the Workers Party on television, emphasizing rural problems and recalling the struggle of Chico Mendes. Three actors—Paulo Betti, Cristina Pereira and José Wilker—appeared on the program. They talked about people who were threatened with death. One of the photographs that appeared on the screen was mine.

Amiraldo and Joana d'Arc, two friends from Minas Gerais, came to visit. Amiraldo said that he had seen a skeleton on the road to Floresta.

"Expedito told me about bodies found there," I told him. "He said that he even sent reports to the mayor. It would be useful to take pictures. Could you take me there?"

"Certainly. I have a Canon camera with me."

We went out in their car. Before reaching the road to Floresta, we left Joana d'Arc at a ranch where she wanted to visit friends.

We parked the car and went into the woods. Behind a fallen tree we found a pile of bones. On top of the tree trunk we saw a black shoe with a red lining. It looked to be of good quality. We went around to the other side of the tree and saw another shoe with a sock and foot bones inside it. Beneath the bones on the ground was a partially disintegrated white shirt with two bullet holes.

Amiraldo bent over and examined the skull. "Strong teeth, of an adult. Maybe 40 years old. He must have been a robust man." He showed me two broken teeth. "One shot in the mouth. Look here." He turned over the skull. "It went out behind."

He took thirteen pictures at different angles, using a flash. The trees with all their dense foliage made the surroundings dark.

On our return, we left the main road to get Joana d'Arc. The house was not far. As we reached the porch I was surprised to see Chico Macedo. I then remembered that I had been to this ranch before. In 1986 the Pastoral Land Commission assisted a union representative who reported the detention of a group of farm workers on a ranch belonging to the Macedo family. The Military Police, accompanied by a lawyer and a church agent, went in and freed the workers.

Chico recognized me and gave me a hug. His parents greeted me without at first remembering me. Despite Chico's hug, there was a certain tension in the air. In the course of the conversation someone mentioned the name of another priest.

"He's a good person," said I.

"Inoffensive," said Chico.

"A good person," I repeated.

"Inoffensive," Chico insisted, giving me a look that implied that I was not.

Since we were all from Minas, we could not dispense with coffee and food. At the table Chico asked me about land occupations.

"Why are the invasions diminishing? The Pastoral Land Commission, although I know you won't agree, is still inciting the farmers."

I laughed. "In fact, I cannot agree. What incites them is hunger, need and Brazil's economic policy. We advise the farmers when they are evicted or threatened with eviction."

"Now you're doing propaganda for the PT. I saw you on television yesterday."

"Look, Chico, I didn't know that they were going to use my picture or raise the subject of death threats."

3.

February 5 to May 5, 1989

Father Ricardo gets into the routine of parish work in a rural town, from everyday pastoral issues to the difficulty of navigating unpaved roads during the rainy season. Expedito receives a death threat.

Sunday, February 5. Yesterday a farmer and his daughter came to the parish house. The girl looked timid. The farmer looked angry enough to breathe fire.

"I want to get the girl married," he said.

I explained that I would need to talk with the young couple, to verify if there was any impediment, and that they should participate in a marriage course. They could do this course in March in Xinguara or in April in Rio Maria.

"No," said the farmer. "The marriage must take place soon. The girl is pregnant. Four months! I'm going to Araguaxim after the boy. He did the job, so he has to marry her."

I explained that a church marriage is valid only if there is free will. There cannot be a marriage by force.

"There won't be any problem," he said. "The boy's father is my brother. He'll order him to marry."

I was wasting my breath and my time. He stood firm in his position and left for Araguaxim.

After the children's mass, I went to visit Dona Geraldina. José Alves was also there.

I asked him about Dona Albina, Belchior's[1] widow. She is now living with Deusdete, a gold prospector.

"Yesterday a peon went to their house," said José Alves. "He attacked Deusdete, injuring him."

"Whenever anyone comes here asking for my sons," said Dona Geral-

---

1. Belchior Martins da Costa, assassinated March 2, 1982.

15

dina, "I say that they're not home. If they ask where they are, I say that I don't know."

I gave Dona Geraldina thirty-four more letters from France and a copy of the two-volume report from Amnesty International on Rural Violence with Impunity.

When I got back to the parish house a man from the countryside was waiting for me. I gave him information about the visits that the pastoral team will be making to base communities in his area next month. He expressed concern about the number of farmers leaving his area. "The ranchers are buying up the land. The farmers clear their plots, but don't have the means to work them. So they sell them." He is planning to move to town himself. For six years he has been working the land of a friend, who has now sold it. He has to move right after the rice harvest.

Monday, February 6. This afternoon the house was filled with people talking about land problems. Expedito was describing the current conflicts.

"Here in this municipal district there are the Redenção and Suaçuí ranches, claimed by the Braga brothers. These ranches were occupied last August by about forty families."

He also talked about the Três Rios Ranch, part of which has been sold. The remaining twelve hundred acres are being disputed between forty *posseiros* and a bank. The owner had used the land as security for a loan and defaulted.

Tonight we had a meeting of the Liturgy Team to prepare for Ash Wednesday. One of the men expressed concern about criticism from the Pentecostals. "They claim that we adore images."

For years we study theology, but what comes up in pastoral work are questions that we thought had been resolved. Clodovis Boff says that to do theology is to respond to the questions of the people. The criticisms by Pentecostals push us back two thousand years to issues raised by the Pharisees.

Sunday, April 9. Rio Maria. Before evening mass, Aldenita, former Mayor Laranjeira's sister, introduced me to two women who are the new public prosecutors, the first ones in this region. One of them has come to work in the court of Xinguara, the other in Rio Maria. During the homily I made reference to their presence in the church and expressed the hope that they will help to establish justice here.

At lunch today Sister Lourdes mentioned a conflict between *posseiros* and a rancher.

"There is a rumor that the rancher received an unsigned threatening note." Lourdes smiled mischievously. "The word going around town is that you wrote the note and that you had organized the farmers to invade his land."

"Then I must have magical powers that I didn't know about. There I was recovering from surgery two thousand kilometers away, and at the same time was here, promoting land occupations and writing threats."

"Well, don't worry," she said laughing. "Now they're saying that the letter was written by Luzia Canuto."

Monday, April 10. Antônio Vieira, the teacher, came to see me with two requests. He wanted to borrow the parish hall for meetings of the PT (Workers' Party) and for the Municipal Conference of Educational Workers, and he wanted me to speak at the latter. I told him that he could borrow the hall for the conference, but should look for another place for the PT meeting. If they met in the church it would help neither the party nor the church. People are already saying that I organized the party. I also suggested that he invite Heloisa or Míriam[2] as a speaker, since they work in the area of grassroots education.

Thursday, April 13. Expedito parked his bicycle outside the parish house. He was smiling, as always. His white shirt and slacks were setting off the dark color of his skin.

"Ricardo," he said, suddenly more serious, "Dimas, the pilot from Redenção, went to the Land Reform Ministry, accusing me of organizing a meeting with farmers, telling them that the Céu Azul Ranch was liberated and that they could go in. He also claimed to have received handwritten threats written on the cover of a copy of the Land Statute. He wants to get a warrant from the judge to search the union office to find out whose handwriting it was."

We went into the house for coffee.

"I just spoke with Neto, the young gunman who lives across the street from me," said Expedito. "He told me that Dimas's men want to kill me."

"How is your relationship with Neto, Expedito?"

"It's good. I've known him since he was a kid."

One of Dona Geraldina's sons came to get the latest pile of letters. I gave him fifteen from Australia, twenty-three from France, one from Germany and two from Portugal.

Tuesday, April 18. A little before Father Pedro das Neves left this parish to move to Xinguara he created the parish land team. Today was my first meeting with them. Present were Antônio Vieira, Dona Francisca, Leontina, Edmundo and Sister Lucila. We had a lively discussion about the team's purpose. Each person said what he or she thought, and I wrote it down. We finally got something together.

2. Míriam Furtado de Mendonça, along with Heloisa Andrade, works for the Basic Education Movement, a church-sponsored grassroots education program in Conceição do Araguaia – tr.

The Land Team should orient the rural workers in the use of the land; visit them; in the more dire cases offer them food and clothing; help with organization and the development of consciousness; deepen their faith; celebrate the lives of the farmers in liturgy.

We agreed that the team is not a union, but should encourage the farmers to organize unions, residents' associations and cooperative work efforts. Before ending our meeting, we chose some dates for specific activities: Workers' Day, Farmers' Day, Diocesan Meeting for Areas of Conflict. We'll ask the Pastoral Land Commission about sending someone to talk about alternative agriculture.

Friday, April 21. Sister Nehida, Sister Lourdes and I left at 8:30 this morning to visit the rural base communities in Lower Rio Maria. As we drove, the noises that the old Toyota jeep was making sounded like complaints about the state of the road. It took us four and a half hours to travel only twenty-eight kilometers. The bridges were shaky, and we nearly went off one of them. The ravines were overflowing, creating plenty of mud. The jeep got stuck three times. Each time, Sister Lourdes would get under the jeep, cheerfully crawling in the mud. By the time we got to Santa Luzia, she was filthy from her blond head to her feet.

The community had not gathered. Given the road conditions, they assumed that we had cancelled our visit.

Monday, April 24. Yesterday after evening mass I took a bus to Redenção, in order to catch a plane to Goiânia for a meeting of the national directorate of the Pastoral Land Commission. I left Rio Maria on a full bus, with a lot of people standing, and gave my seat to a woman with two children. Then the good stretch of road ended. As the vehicle swayed and bounced around enormous potholes, I kept trying to find a less uncomfortable position. I was soon feeling pain in every part of my body. I was also feeling outrage at public officials for their neglect of the roads and bridges. The only time they show up is when they want to collect taxes or persecute the poor. At the Salobro River we had to get off the bus because the bridge was out. Another bus was waiting on the other side. We had to cross the river by walking on pieces of wood loosely joined together, carrying our bags and guided in the darkness only by the bus's headlights.

Monday, May 1. The first meeting of the Public Education Workers of Rio Maria was held in the parish hall. Antônio insisted that I address the group. Luzia Canuto, who is a teacher, was there. I gave her seventeen letters addressed to her mother from France, Italy and Norway.

Friday, May 5. On Tuesday Sister Lourdes and I traveled to the São José base community in a fine rain, battling mud holes all the way. We did forty kilometers in the jeep and eleven on foot. Walking that distance would not have been difficult, if it hadn't been for the rain, the mud and our baggage. At one point my feisty companion sank into the mud almost to her waist. She managed to get out, but without one of her sandals. It was hard work finding it.

We celebrated mass in the home of Francisco and Laura, who served us lunch. A lot of people were absent because they thought that the bad roads would keep us away.

Early Thursday morning, we set out for the home of Pelé and Neusa, and got there without any serious problems. Neusa had prepared a mouth-watering stewed chicken. While we were having lunch two tired-looking peons came to the door. We invited them to help themselves to the food. They told us that they were going back to Rio Maria, after having worked on a ranch without being paid.

When the meal was over, we walked over to the school where we would be celebrating mass. There was good participation in both the hymns and the reflections. After the celebration the people auctioned a live hen, which the buyer then presented to me.

We continued our journey, now with the hen. On the way to the Conselho community we saw a young man whom I had previously met when he was among those arrested during the conflict over the Canaan Ranch. I had visited them several times in jail. Later the ranch was expropriated and a large number of people, including João Canuto and Expedito, got land.

Before mass we went to visit Jesuino. Some years ago he was a *posseiro* in Xinguara, when a violent land conflict erupted. The rancher claiming the land killed a farmer, and many others fled in fear. As the situation became dangerous, Jesuino was forced to abandon his plot of land. His present house is in a beautiful spot, surrounded by sesame, cassava and palm trees. Behind it is a small stream, where some pigs were cooling themselves.

I asked Jesuino, "Don't the neighbors who live farther down the stream use this water for drinking and bathing?"

"Yes, but by the time the water gets there it's already filtered."

The houses are only about five hundred yards apart.

That night we stayed with Divino. I went down to the stream, taking along an oil wick that produced more smoke than light. It was dark and the ground was slippery. I hung my clothes on the branches of a bush and stepped into the cold water. As I took my bath I thought of the pigs upstream.

The next day we went to the Bom Jesus community, where Francisco das Chagas and his wife had lunch ready for us. The area where they live used to be the Marajoara Ranch, the location of a violent conflict. After the farmers received permission from the Land Reform Ministry to occupy the land, they put up their houses and planted their fields. Then the ministry revoked the permission and the rancher began shooting at them and destroying their homes and fields. I was there several times in those days. Now I was sad to see that of the original settlers only two remained. Most people left because of the lack of a school, a road and medical facilities. The government grants people land, but doesn't provide an infrastructure or any technical assistance to enable them to stay on it.

There were only thirty-five people, including children, at mass. Partway through, it began to rain. People were worried about the bean crop, which could rot if there was no pause in the rain.

We left right after mass, driving through enormous puddles of water. After only fifty yards the jeep got stuck.

4.

May 7 to May 31, 1989

A regional gathering of the Pastoral Land Commission becomes an occasion for more reminiscences because of the presence of Dona Olinda, mother of the slain priest Father Josimo Morais Tavares. When Ricardo returns to Rio Maria, there is news of growing violence around the land occupation at the Suaçui Ranch, owned by Geraldo de Oliveira Braga (nicknamed "Braguinha"). Accounts of past and recent brutality fill in the picture of difficulties experienced by poor people who have come to Rio Maria seeking a better life.

Sunday, May 7. I drove to Conceição do Araguaia. There I met up with Aninha and Guaracy and went with them to Miracema, for the regional assembly of the Pastoral Land Commission.

Dona Olinda participated in the Assembly. We sat and talked on the veranda of the Training Center.

"I got married very young," said the thin woman in her gentle voice. "I was only 14 years old when Josimo was born on the shore of the river in Marabá. I was alone, washing clothes, when I felt the pains. I didn't have time to get help or to get home.

"Josimo finished his studies when he was 24 years old, but they thought he was too young to be ordained. So he had to wait one more year."

Three years ago, Josimo, dedicated missionary, poet and friend of mine, was assassinated in Imperatriz, Maranhão.

Dom Pedro Casaldáliga was present at the mass celebrating the anniversary of the Araguaia-Tocantins region of the Pastoral Land Commission. At the kiss of peace, he made it a point to embrace Dona Olinda first.

Freely cherish your dreams
That are the dreams of this people.
Carve with tenderness
and a keen knife the stars

21

and open your breast.
Immerse yourself in the crystalline streams,
pass through the dense forests of *babaçu* palms,
where plants are rooted and people are uprooted.

Come in the spring, gathering flowers,
and bring them.
Recite the last poem that you wrote;
sing the version that has not yet been sung.
Come. Come!
Raimunda, Bertoldo,
Nicole and Nicola, José,
Carlinhos, Domingos,
Lourdinha, Goreth, Mada and Bia,
are all waiting.

Dona Olinda dries her tears
with a corner of her apron.
The wind sways the flags,
the accordionist draws out the first notes,
the guitars are tuned,
the nut-harvesters[1]
gather their baskets,
the farmers put away their tools.

Everyone bathes in the spring.
The young girls put on their make-up
and dress in Sunday clothes.
The chapel is full.
The children are quiet,
waiting for you.
Above the altar are containers of earth and water,
the chalice with red wine, the color of blood,
the bread broken, shared, of the body,
in the alliance that today is permanent,
forged in times of pain.

Look, Josimo,
at these hands that held you;
at these eyes that watched you.

1. It is a custom for women in Maranhão and northern Tocantins to gather the nuts of the *babaçu* palm tree, break the hard shells and sell the contents to be processed into oil. The breaking of the shells is exhausting work, but is done to supplement the families' livelihood — tr.

The feast begins today
and thus you come, bathed and purified,
in the blood of the Lamb,
laughing, proud, happy
because you awakened our dreams.

Saturday, May 13. Rio Maria. Anniversary of the city. We were awakened by the deafening noise of fireworks and fanfares. Mayor Tião Aranha asked me to bless the new courthouse and to be present at the installation of the new judge.

This was the first time that I was called to bless a public establishment. Many authorities, soldiers of the Military Police and civilians were present. After the national anthem and the hoisting of the flag they handed me the microphone. I invoked the blessing of God and his strength "so that in Rio Maria there will be rights for the poor, for the marginalized, for the gold prospectors, for those without voice. May law and justice walk together; may the martyrs for land contemplate your will."

I left after that. The first speaker after my blessing was Eronides de Souza Primo, judge of Conceição do Araguaia. As I was walking away I could hear his voice through the loudspeaker, saying that when he came to the district court there were more than a thousand cases pending, and that he worked very hard.

"If there are people dissatisfied with me, it is because the law isn't made to please everybody!"

He neglected to say that in all those years he did not hold a single trial for the murders of dozens of small farmers, but was generous with the big landowners. He signed orders allowing for violent evictions, burnings of homes and the torture of farmers.

"I am a servant of the law!" he cried.

Tell that to the landless farmers.

Monday, May 22. Seu[2] Antônio, a white-haired man from Minas Gerais who prays the rosary daily and listens to the diocesan radio station, has a fatherly affection for all the priests who have served in the parish. Today he left his rural community in Araguaxim to come talk with me.

"Last year about forty men began to occupy land at Suaçuí. Braguinha, the rancher, made an agreement with those who had already planted fields. But then he brought in four gunmen. They shot one man while he was sleeping. Then they killed a man of seventy. The rest of the workers fled. Now there are three gunmen guarding the entrance to the ranch. Everyone is afraid to pass by there."

I suggested that he get together with others who know about these incidents, and register a complaint at the police station. Seu Antônio looked at me sadly.

2. "Seu" is the term of respect preceding the given name of an older man — tr.

"The police know. They ordered that the old man be buried. But they didn't do anything else."

I went to talk with Expedito. He confirmed what Seu Antônio had told me. He also said that one of the farmers had been on the land for eight years.

"He had a hundred sacks of rice, and each sack was worth sixty new cruzeiros. He had pigs. A lot of things. They pressured him to accept only ten thousand new cruzeiros. There were other farmers who got nothing."

Then Expedito told me that he was being sued for libel.

"By whom?" I asked, surprised.

"The rancher Dimas, because of an interview that I gave for a newspaper from Belém."

Tuesday, May 23. The renovations of the church will have to be stopped. The contractor underestimated the quantity of material and the prices.

The wall behind the altar is now yellow. The other walls are white. Sister Lourdes doesn't like the color scheme. She says that white and yellow don't go well together. I spoke with my friend Manelão, who is an artist.

"But yellow and white do go together," said Manelão, "very well." He scratched his thin beard and smiled. "Maybe Sister Lourdes doesn't like them because they are the colors of the Vatican."

At the end of the day Expedito came over. He was carrying a large notebook containing his poems and some union papers. He took off his cap and began reading.

Death

1. Death is a black stroke/From which I cannot escape,
   It has a well-made noose,/It throws only to catch.
   The river of life/Carries us toward death.

3. Death entered the world/Through the sin of Adam.
   We are his descendants./We fall into the trap,
   We follow our parents/And move toward the knife.

9. One may be famous/One may be comely
   One may have wealth,/Prestige and power,
   But all will be left/On the bed of the tomb.

22. We cannot scorn death,/Nor scorn its reach,
    It comes, carrying us all/Believer or atheist,
    Carrying us all the way/To Jesus, Son of God.

Thursday, May 25. After evening mass a small property owner came looking for me, worried.

"Last night I was with Ceará, in front of the *Bate-Papo* bar. He told me that he and three other farmers from Suaçuí had refused Braguinha's offer for their land and were threatened with death. Braguinha's men have already killed one of them. I had told him to hide, but he didn't think that he'd be killed in town."

Right after I heard this news Dona Maria came in very upset. She told me that during mass she asked herself whether the gate in front of the parish house was locked or only closed. She left the church to check. She pushed open the gate and saw the two doors of the jeep open and a man at each door.

"They were arguing," she said. "With the noise that I made, they left running."

Sister Lourdes, Sister Nehida, two other people and I had been planning to leave after mass for Conceição do Araguaia, where we were going to attend a course on the New Constitution. Now that seemed unwise, especially at night. Someone could ambush us along the road. I consulted the others. We decided that we should still go to Conceição, in order to discuss the situation with Bishop Hanrahan and with our friends at the Pastoral Land Commission, but that we should leave closer to dawn. Sister Lourdes insisted that we leave by 3 A.M., which would allow us to get to Conceição shortly after 8, so that we would not be late for the course.

Sunday, May 28. After talking with the bishop, and with Aninha, Guaracy and other people from the Pastoral Land Commission, I decided to go back to Rio Maria in order to give support to Ceará's widow and get more information. Guaracy came with me. Before we left, Aninha told me that a friend had heard some ranchers saying, "The solution to the land problems is to kill Raimundo Marques, Valter Peixoto, Aninha and Father Ricardo." A few hours later another friend was in a bar, where he saw those same men and heard the same things.

Today I went with Expedito and Guaracy to visit Lígia, Ceará's widow. She looked like a child, with her thin little body and big dark eyes, as she sat outside the house playing with her two small sons. She seemed to be communicating very well with them, which she cannot do with adults. Lígia is deaf. We talked with her mother, Dona Benvinda.

"Ceará caught two bullets," said Dona Benvinda. "He was sitting in front of the house, with the two little boys in his arms. My daughter saw everything. They killed him and pushed Lígia into the house."

"Dona Benvinda, what was Ceará's full name?" Guaracy asked.

"Zeferino Francisco de Oliveira."

"Have his relatives been told?" asked Expedito.

"No. We don't know their address. But I remember that he had a nephew in Araguaína."

Monday, May 29. We still had not been able to find out the name of the other man who was killed. Perhaps Ferreti, one of the other farmers being threatened, would know.

Guaracy was late for lunch. Finally he arrived with Ferreti, who was looking worried.

"I talked with Ceará a little before he was killed," he said. "He talked about the threats. I don't want to die. I'm married and have two children. I learned about the death of one farmer and now Ceará. Those people don't threaten only to frighten. You have to sleep with one eye open."

We suggested that he register a complaint with the police, but he doesn't trust the authorities. Neither do the others. The government has never done anything to make them trust it.

Murder is a long-standing custom in this town. In 1977 there was an ugly dispute over the division of land for ranches. There were murders on both sides, totalling about twenty. The conflict ended when one of the ranchers killed one of his enemy's gunmen, pulled the skin off his face and nailed it to the gate of the ranch.

That same year one of these ranchers hired a peon who took a fancy to his manager's wife. So the rancher authorized the manager to put an end to the peon. The manager beat him to death, threw him into a 200-liter drum, boiled him and fed him to the pigs.

During the time when Seabra was police chief there wasn't a night without a killing, mainly because of robbery. Seabra himself was accused of killing a gold dealer. In 1985 he went to some ranchers and proposed hiring thirty gunmen who would be at their service under his command, but the idea didn't get off the ground.

That reminded me of the "security companies" that appeared that year. In January 1986 a newspaper in Rio de Janeiro printed an interview with the Secretary of Public Safety of the state of Mato Grosso that revealed that sixteen hundred soldiers had left the army and joined private militias, where they earned three times their previous salary.

Wednesday, May 31. I went back to Conceição do Araguaia for the Diocesan Council meeting and for a retreat with Father Luís Mosconi, who teaches our seminarians in Belém. This retreat is a time of silence, a moment for examining our fragilities, our contradictions. We are challenged to hear with the ears of the Lord. We are invited to drink from spiritual vessels.

Mosconi spoke to us of the crisis of spirituality in the church. It must be purified. It must be washed in the waters of conversion and find in Jesus its Lord, its Reason. He approached the gospel from a Latin American perspective, insisting that living the gospel here is not the same as living it in Europe, Asia or Africa.

Angels of the Night

There are little children
who are angels of the night,

Shadowy birds in the darkness.
Little children from harsh poverty fly
through the streets of Recife and alight on the sidewalks
                                    and beneath bridges.

The child-angels of the streets
are noisy, thin, with visible bones,
eyes ablaze, as
they avidly devour the smell of glue
in their desperate search for a respite from hunger,
for a fleeting moment in a world of enchantment,
when the angel is clothed in light and
becomes a dazzling bird.

Little children, hunters of dreams,
starved for bread and affection,
perform acrobatics in the air,
displaying their dreams on the avenue.

Recife sleeps lazily
and a child recites an impassioned verse
and begs Aninha to write it on the ground, quickly,
before the inspiration is gone.

Recife sleeps lazily
and a child wakes, his face covered with alcohol
and touched by flame.

Recife sleeps.

But awake are the transvestite, with lost eyes,
and the black prostitute,
wrapped in the same drama, dread, destiny, insanity,
staring with the eyes of night at the burning child.

The angel of the night at this hour
flies low.

Recife sleeps.

On the sidewalk, naked, lies the dying bird,
lies the nation.

5.

June 2 to June 28, 1989

After the sadness in the story of Dona Olinda and Father Josimo, the complexity of life in Rio Maria reaches a point of being almost amusing. There are tensions between ecological concerns and the acceptance of people's way of life, between faith and politics, between murder and religious conversion. Neto, the nineteen-year-old gunman who is hated and feared by almost everyone in town, is shown in a different light.

Friday, June 2. Yesterday I was in Goiânia with Dona Olinda, Father Josimo's mother. She brought charges against the state and federal governments, holding them responsible for the murder of her son, and requested a pension equivalent to two minimum salaries (about $200 per month). Also giving testimony were Dom Antônio Ribeiro, Archbishop of Goiânia, and Dom Aloísio Pinto Hilário, Bishop of Tocantinópolis.

We told the judge that the authorities knew about the death threats but remained indifferent. Father Josimo himself filed a complaint with the police after the attempt on his life in April 1986 and wrote a report, which he sent to the authorities and to the press. The diocese of Tocantinópolis also sent letters to the authorities. A committee of which I was a member had an audience on April 30 of that year with President Sarney. We told him about the climate of violence in the region and the attempt on Josimo's life. Archbishop Luciano Mendes spoke to the minister of justice. I went to see the minister of agrarian reform. The archbishop of Goiânia met with the governor of Goiás. On May 10, after all our efforts, a gunman named Geraldo Rodrigues da Costa killed Josimo.

I flew back to the south of Pará in a small, single-engine plane. As we passed over the Araguaia river, I was enjoying the sight of the beaches along the edges and on tiny islands in the middle. The devastated areas of the forest looked like wounds.

Turtle Fate

Oneide told me
that in Santana do Araguaia
she went running along the beaches,
as she happily gathered more
than a thousand turtle eggs.

Happy was she as she spoke,
sad was I,
thinking about the eggs,
thinking about the turtles,
as they faced their tragic lot
in Oneide's cooking pot.

Monday, June 12. Rio Maria. On Saturday I went to the São Pedro base community to preside over a wedding. The family had prepared some bamboo arches, winding colored paper around them, for the couple to pass under. Just before the wedding a heavy rain destroyed all their work. They did it all over again.

The couple was wearing rented clothing. The big problem was tying the necktie. No one knew how, so they called me to help. I didn't really know how to do it, but I improvised. Finally we began the ceremony, an hour late. The young man came in smiling, with the tie hanging outside the jacket, because no one wanted it hidden.

One of the guests persuaded me to take a different route home, saying that it had less mud and fewer holes. Besides, I could give a ride to his parents, who live on that road. When we got to their home, a tiny little hut built of mud and wattle, the mother wanted to prepare supper, but I told her I was in a hurry. So she ran out to the yard, grabbed a live hen and gave it to me.

Thursday, June 15. I just learned that Seu Vicente, a medium-sized-property owner, was murdered at the entrance of his farm by bandits who escaped in his car. Seu Vicente was a good man, peaceable and loved by many people. He always came to mass with his family.

Sister Lourdes and I visited Seu Vicente's family. Everyone was crying. Outside the house some men were talking. One of them said that he heard an attorney at the courthouse saying that it's time that a leader die for the region to calm down.

"Canuto died; things calmed down. Paulo Fonteles died; the situation was calmer."

Some people believe that he was suggesting that Expedito should die.

Sunday, June 18. I just got back from a trip to the countryside and learned about the arrest, for the murder of Seu Vicente, of Sebastião, a notorious gunman and car thief.

Rage spread through town, and people began talking about lynching. I was worried. On Saturday afternoon a crowd accompanied the body of Seu Vicente to the church.

"So many people," said Dona Maria in astonishment. "Even on top of the benches."

Later Dona Maria told me what happened after the burial.

"Some men armed with pieces of wood, iron rods and guns invaded the police station and killed Sebastião. They dragged his body into the street, kicking and stomping on it. Adults and children participated, laughing. There were important people of the city encouraging the lynching."

Were they taking advantage of the anger of the people in order to eliminate someone who might incriminate others?

Neto, the young gunman, was also in jail at the same time as Sebastião. Someone influential intervened so that he was freed before the lynching.

Monday, June 19. I was talking with a friend about the lynching. He told me, "I think it was good. The gunman had to meet that end, because the unrest was too much."

"But is that right?" I asked him. "For a lot of reasons I don't agree with what happened. Don't you find it strange to attack the fruit when the sickness is in the tree? To put an end to car thefts and murders, wouldn't it have been better to save the life of Sebastião, who might have been a key person in unraveling this whole crime web?"

My friend ended up agreeing. But I was dismayed to hear his reasoning.

"They could have waited another month, and, gradually, if they stuck things under his fingernails, he would have revealed everything."

While we were talking, in came Seu Miguel, a bricklayer who has been working on the church and who is a member of the Assembly of God. He had news about Neto, the gunman. Seu Miguel was looking very happy.

"Yesterday in our church Neto dedicated himself to Jesus."

Tuesday, June 20. Expedito came to the parish house. I lowered the volume on an album of Chico Buarque that I had been listening to.

"Neto was at my house yesterday. He told me that he got religion. He also told me that he killed 'only five men,' but he 'helped to kill eighteen.' He described some of the crimes. He talked about a man that his group killed in the market place. When the job was done, one of the partners wanted to take the victim's money. Neto wouldn't allow that. 'If you take it, they'll think that we killed him for robbery.' "

"Expedito, what is Neto's full name?" I asked.

"Manoel Barbosa Milhomem. He was named for his grandfather. He is the son of Maria Barbosa Milhomem and Valdemar Pereira Milhomem. His father works as a peon."

"Since you've known Neto since he was a little boy, explain to me how he became a gunman."

"He learned it from ranchers and cowhands when he and his brother Marivaldo went out to work on the ranches. Neto was 14 years old, Marivaldo 15."

Just then Brás came into the parish house. He is an auto mechanic who is openly supportive of the Union of Rural Workers. During the recent elections Brás was a candidate for town council. On the campaign flyers he presented himself as *THE PHILANTHROPIC CANDIDATE*, promising to divide his salary among social assistance projects, the Communist Party and the Catholic church. He wasn't elected.

Brás mentioned that he had heard that Neto's brother Marivaldo was arrested in Mato Grosso.

"Three months ago," said Expedito, "a man with a big thirty-eight invaded the house of Seu Valdemar, wanting to get Neto, who slipped away through the backyard. The guy, seeing that he had lost his chance, grabbed Neto's mother as a shield and, keeping his gun pointed against her head, stepped out of the house. It was the biggest commotion ever seen on our street. Neto was waiting in ambush, but wouldn't shoot so as not to hit his mother."

"When Neto was in jail," said Brás, "he wrote on the wall 'Big Neto the Killer! A sharp guy takes pride in his profession!' "

I arranged with Expedito to attend a meeting at the Pastoral Land Commission about the program for Farmers' Day and about the Alternative Agriculture Conference to be held in Redenção.

Wednesday, June 21. Dona Maria told me that a farmer from the São José base community had come to tell me about another death in the region. I asked Dona Maria the reason for the murder.

"Going too far in another man's family."

"What do you mean, 'going too far,' Dona Maria?"

"The craziness of fooling around with another man's wife."

Later on I was near the São Miguel gas station talking with some friends. One of them called me aside.

"That one over there at the table, with the red shirt and the cap, is Neto."

I looked. A few yards away, sitting casually on a chair, was a thin young man talking with other youths. I had heard that Neto was light-haired, but that this week he dyed his hair and his eyebrows black.

"He tried it as a disguise," said my friend, "but it doesn't work."

Saturday, June 23. Expedito returned from Conceição, where he gave testimony in the libel suit brought against him by Dimas. He told me that during the interrogation the lawyer for the rancher spoke in a sarcastic tone.

"In spite of the prayers of Father Ricardo, Rio Maria has gotten worse. The number of invasions has increased."

Then he began to interrogate Expedito with regard to my relationship with the union.

Expedito replied that I had my specific work and the union its own.

Expedito and I talked about the bodies that had appeared in Bambuzal. He said he would sound out Neto about those murders.

Sunday, June 25. Today we began a Bible course in the main church. As a starting point, we listened to people's questions, doubts and anxieties. Many of their issues arise in contact with the Pentecostal churches, who have no use for interfaith dialogue.

We talked about faith and how it is important to know how to explain the reasons for one's own faith. To have more knowledge, however, does not necessarily mean to be more faithful to the Gospel. Jesus spoke sharply to the doctors of the law, warning them that sinners and prostitutes would precede them into the Kingdom.

Monday, June 26. This week Expedito visited the Três Rios community. On the bus back he rode beside a farmer who was pointing out locations of corpses.

"Behind that log there's a pile of bones," said the farmer. "There someone is poorly buried, with hair showing; two more over there. In the pasture there's another one."

The first sounded like the one that I saw with Amiraldo and that he photographed.

"I checked with Neto," said Expedito. "He told me that he killed a well-dressed peon, who had come from Marabá looking for him. He, his Uncle Porfírio and Peixoto went after him. Later they threw the body near the road to Floresta. Neto also said that the other bodies in that location were the work of the late Sebastião, of Peixoto and of his brother Marivaldo."

Wednesday, June 28. Roberto[1] and Doza, both of the Communist Party, came to see me. Roberto wanted to know whether I was inclined to discuss the subject of the presidential election. Doza, with his glasses in his shirt pocket and newspapers under his arm, remained silent as he sank into the chair of woven plastic. I made it clear that I support Lula[2] for president, but that I don't want to get officially involved in the campaign, so as not to mix the church with the party. On an informal level, however, I'm willing to discuss the issues.

1. Roberto Neto da Silva is one of the few founders of the Union of Rural Workers of Rio Maria who is still alive—tr.

2. Luís Inácio da Silva, president of the Workers' Party (PT) and candidate for president of Brazil—tr.

6.

July 9 to August 27, 1989

A son and son-in-law of João Canuto are suddenly arrested by the local police. There is no evidence of their having committed the crime with which they are charged, the murder of an employee of the Suaçuí Ranch.

Descriptions of visits to rural base communities give a sense of the religious and social context of the lives of farmers in the south of the state of Pará.

Sunday, July 9. I went out early in the morning to buy bread and saw Expedito with the sons and nephews of Canuto outside the church. I was in a hurry because of mass but stopped to say hello. I learned to my horror that the police had arrested Orlando and Carlos at eleven o'clock last night without any judicial order. The police chief claims that they are charged with the murder of one of Braguinha's men.

During the children's mass I worried about the arrest. Afterward I went to the police station and managed to talk with Carlos and Orlando through the barred window. Then I went with Carlos's wife, Luzia, to the home of Aldenita, the sister of former Mayor Laranjeira, with whom the public prosecutor, Doctor Eunice, is staying. We told the prosecutor about the irregular situation of the arrest. She listened in silence. Then she told us to go speak to the police chief. I insisted that she speak to him herself and offered to drive her. She refused. So I asked her to send him a written message. She went to her room, then came back saying that she didn't have any paper. Finally she agreed to go with us to the station. She promised me that Carlos and Orlando would have an immediate hearing and would be freed.

When we found the police chief he said that he understood my arguments, but that he was going to wait for the judge to decide.

"They should be freed now," I insisted, "even if the judge were coming tomorrow, because there is no legal basis for this."

"I will question Carlos," said the chief. "Then I will meet with the prosecutor."

"I expect the two of them to sleep at home tonight," I said as the chief and the prosecutor disappeared into an inner room. When they finished talking Doctor Eunice refused my offer of a ride and left in the police car.

I stopped in front of the window of the cell to talk with Orlando. He was in a bad mood. He asked me to bring him a blanket and some clothes.

"Taking a bath without changing clothes," he said, "is like shitting without wiping your ass."

He had reason to complain. The jail is small and crowded, hot during the day and cold at night, and there are never enough blankets.

I invited Luzia and Carlos's brother José to go with me to talk with Doctor Eunice again. She looked surprised to see us.

"We aren't here to ask for privileges," I told her. "We're here to demand justice. The arrest is illegal."

"There are charges against them," she argued. "If they are set free they'll run away."

"Doctor, they have known, regular addresses. Besides, even if, hypothetically, they had committed one or more murders, they have the right to respond in liberty. This is in clear violation of the Constitution that's just been passed."

She didn't say anything, so I continued.

"People from various parts of the world are mobilizing, demanding the investigation of the murder of João Canuto, and here they arrest his son and his son-in-law!"

"Doctor Eunice," said Luzia, "this same chief arrested my father in 1984. And when he was assassinated, the chief didn't arrest the gunmen, claiming that there was no court order. Carlos knew where they were hiding, but the police didn't do anything."

"In light of what Luzia has just told you," I said, "this chief does not have the neutrality needed to lead an investigation. Besides, even when Neto was arrested, he was inexplicably freed."

The prosecutor glared at me. "There are land problems here. These are people who invade land."

"I know about the land problems," I replied. "But how many farmers have been arrested in recent years? Hundreds. And gunmen? Hardly any. Gunmen have killed more than a hundred fifty farmers in the past nine years. There is clear bias in the exercise of justice, Doctor."

At that point Aldenita brought in some juice. She told me that she is a friend of Father Leonardo Boff. I told her that I know him well, too.

"When do the charismatics meet?" asked Doctor Eunice.

"Every Wednesday," I replied.

"In Belém I belonged to a charismatic group," she said.

Before leaving I went back to prodding her on the subject of the prisoners.

"I hope that justice will be done, that the law will be applied. In the name of law, in the name of God, Judge of the judges and of prosecutors, the two should sleep at home tonight."

Before the evening mass I learned that Orlando and Carlos were still in jail. When I saw the prosecutor in church, I sent someone to the police station to get Luzia. After mass I met with Luzia and with Carlos's brothers. Unfortunately Doctor Eunice got away. I decided to go talk with the police chief. I reminded him that Carlos and Orlando had not been caught in any crime and that there was no judicial order justifying their arrest.

Monday, July 10. Carlos and Orlando slept at home last night. Today Orlando came over with Roberto. They told me that a farmer from Canaan had joined the occupation at Suaçuí, but, when the time came for negotiating, he betrayed his companions and took the side of Braguinha.

This afternoon I drove to Redenção to meet Günther's plane. Günther belongs to a non-governmental organization in Germany, called *Brasilien Initiative*, which disseminates information about our country and denounces injustice. We became friends in 1985, when I stayed at his home in Freiburg. Today Günther brought greetings from the pastoral team in São Félix do Araguaia, where he had attended the diocesan assembly last week, and from people in Germany. He is thinking of publishing a book about Brazil, and so wants to talk with gold prospectors, farmers and people in grassroots movements.

Tuesday, July 11. Günther and I visited Dona Geraldina. Carlos was there. We still have to get a *habeas corpus* for him and Orlando.

We then visited a nearby mining camp, where Günther took pictures and interviewed some prospectors. He drew laughter by getting his feet stuck in the mud without realizing it.

Wednesday, July 12. I introduced Günther to Expedito, and they talked for a long time. Expedito showed Günther some of his poems and recited his *Tribute to Chico Mendes*:

On that ill-starred day/Nature groaned
All joy disappeared/Brazil was convulsed
The world was jolted/The waters swirled.
The Amazon mourned/The earth was cloaked in grief
When the news was heard/Of the death of Chico Mendes

This sad news/Left the people in shock
By the hand of a gunman/Chico was killed
The union leader/had not made a date
For his execution/In his own home
Chico was shot

He died for the present/But his name becomes history
He was a great fighter/Who lives in the memory
Of the Brazilian people/His companions weep
At the loss of a hero/Bound for glory
His hope of victory/Time will not destroy

In the bed of the grave/I know that he sleeps
With great pleasure and relish/He defended the oppressed
He defended nature/That rich paradise
Was defended by him/He was a great man
And so his name/Will not be forgotten

He was a great fighter/Who loved his country
He struggled so its people/Would have happier days
His story is passed on/He will be remembered
By future generations/In a free land
With a smiling people/In a giant Nation

Günther recorded an interview with Expedito, who gave him copies of some of his poems.

Monday, July 17. I went with Airton to the São Sebastião II community, where Seu Zé Fizico received us. His house is simple but functional. He even installed running water, putting the water tank near a spring, on a higher level than the house. He fills it manually. It supplies the kitchen and the bathroom. Seu Zé is thinking of passing a pipe through the wood stove to get hot water.

Tuesday, July 18. We got to Our Lady Aparecida community at 10 A.M. After parking the jeep we walked to the home of José Almeida, beside the Bananal River, where we will meet tomorrow with the leaders of four neighboring communities for biblical study and prayer. This was where Airton and I would be sleeping. The room had a bed and a mattress on the floor.

That evening we got towels and soap and went to the river. We took a bath beside the bridge, while the first signs of the night shadows were appearing. The waters were flowing strong, pulling us. On our return we found a hen in the bed. When I came closer she fled through the window, making a tremendous racket.

Airton slept on the mattress on the floor, leaving me the bed. Throughout the night a cat and four kittens fought with him over the mattress. At dawn the cat brought a mouse for her kittens.

Wednesday, July 19. We got ready for the Bible course. Zé Almeida brought chairs and stools. We improvised work tables with boards in the shade of the trees.

That afternoon we traveled on horseback with Mário to his home, three and a half kilometers away. We cut through the property of the Bannach family. It's amazing how quickly the abandoned pasture has reverted to brush.

"I came from Morrinhos, in Goiás," said Mário. "My wife had eleven children. God took six."

He pointed out that the forest is untouched. I observed that there wasn't much thick wood.

"I think there was a fire here some years ago," said Mário. "I found charcoal as much as a foot below ground level. Maybe lightning hit the woods one summer. We have been here for three years. We suffered a lot when Bannach did some clearing and threw the wood in the pond, over there, adjoining my land. It rotted and brought malaria. But, thank God, we're living well now." Seu Mário pulled the fence wire aside so that we could pass through. "Our biggest problem is not having roads. Last year Dona Raimunda, the teacher, who was pregnant, got sick with toxemia and had to be carried out in a hammock. During the rainy season! When we got to Santa Cecília, we borrowed an old pickup truck. Dona Raimunda was passing out, and we thought that she was going to die. With all the bumps in the road, she miscarried. We got to town filthy and without money, but managed to get her into the hospital."

We went down a very steep incline. The harness of Airton's horse slipped around its neck. Airton had to get off and do the last stretch on foot. We left the animals beside the stream and crossed the plank bridge carefully, because there was no handrail. A few yards later we came to Mário's little house. It was recently built and has a roof of ceramic tiles.

Mário and his wife Maria Terezinha moved in only yesterday. Everything is clean and beautiful. The yard is filled with fruit trees. Behind the house is a stream of cold water. They wanted to heat the water for our baths, but we refused.

Although the stream is near the house, Mário said that we could bathe nude, promising that the girls would stay out of the backyard. The water was really freezing. We laughed and shivered. Airton courageously lay down in the stream.

"This is cold enough to shrink your weenie!" said Mário.

We had supper in the kitchen, then went to the front room, where there was a deer hide, folded and hanging over a beam. We got to talking about hunting, and laughed at the men's wild exaggerations.

As night fell a beautiful moon appeared behind the trees. The inside of the house was lighted by the weak, trembling flame of an oil wick. The wind was blowing through the house. During the day the heat is suffocating, but at night it's cold because of the nearness of the forest. It was time to sleep, but too cold to use a hammock. They took Airton and me to the bedroom, where there was a large cane bed. If we didn't want to sleep together, they could put a mattress on the floor. The experience with the cats at Zé Almeida's house was the deciding factor.

Friday, August 7. Yesterday when I returned to Rio Maria, Dona Maria couldn't wait to tell me the latest news.

"Neto is back in town. I saw him with my own mortal eyes. He was with two other gunmen over there near the bridge fooling around with some women. He got back a week ago and already killed another gunman."

Yesterday two men tried to shoot Neto, but missed.

Wednesday, August 16. Today we arrived at the São Cristóvão community and slept in the home of Édio and Paz. They have three daughters and a little boy. The house is of wood, painted blue, with the floor more elevated than in the majority of homes. At the back there is a service area with a water tank. Like José Fizico, they have piped in water. They don't have to fill the water tank by hand, however, because the pipes run from a stream above the house.

Édio's nephew Jorge is helping to clear the land. Over coffee he explained how it is done.

"It takes me three days to clear ten acres, cutting the brushwood and the vines. In an area that has already been burned it's twelve days before the field is ready for planting. It's easier to prepare an area that has not been previously burned. The field is ready in eight days. After you've used fire, the brush grows back thicker."[1]

I wanted to visit neighboring residents, but the car wouldn't start for anything. While we were waiting for the sun to warm the engine, we looked at six bird nests hanging from a *conde* tree. On the same branch was an enormous wasp nest.

"Birds and wasps live together well," I observed.

Édio agreed. "When a sparrow hawk tries to attack the birds, the wasps send the intruder running."

We finally got the car going. On the way to our next destination we stopped at a small restaurant. Behind it I found an outhouse. I pulled open the board that served as a door, and went inside. Then I saw the bees. They were coming and going through the cracks in the wood of the floor. I really needed to use the privy, but was hesitating. What if I startled the bees? I finally decided to take my chances and did what I had to without getting stung.

Sunday, August 20. Expedito received a summons from Judge José Cândido Moraes, ordering him to appear for questioning on the *habeas*

1. Most small farmers in Northern Brazil, lacking the economic means to buy fertilizers and tractors, use the traditional slash-and-burn method to prepare the land. The Pastoral Land Commission employs agronomists to help people develop agricultural techniques that are less harmful to the soil and the atmosphere—tr.

corpus for which the union had petitioned for Carlos and Orlando. Since there was no time to contact the lawyer in Belém who had helped with the petition, I offered to go with him. Today, after the children's mass, Expedito and I met with Carlos and Orlando. We discussed the points to be argued in relation to the document by the police chief containing the charges against them. It was not difficult to refute the document. It stated that there was "incontestible evidence" that Orlando and Carlos committed a crime, but, further down, admitted to not having "finished taking statements" and noted that "certain essential steps" had still to be taken.

Expedito smiled. "It looks like the chief prepared things with his hands and undid them with his feet!"

The chief's "evidence" was fragile and based on the statements of a man named Francisco Veloso, who said: "I learned through third parties that the ranch had been recently invaded and that among the invaders were Carlos and Orlando." He did not give the names of these third parties. Also he did not state that these third parties claimed that Carlos and Orlando had killed someone. Furthermore, the statement that Orlando was among the invaders was dubious, since Orlando had never occupied that area. The informant also lied in stating that Carlos had land in Canaan, acquired after an invasion. Carlos had never filed a claim in that area.

The next statement was from someone named Pedro Alcântara. This man spoke about the death of a farmer named Izídio, without saying who killed him, but revealed that, in the place of the crime, there was a twenty-eight-caliber rifle belonging to the gunman Aprígio Menezes.

The chief's final "proof" was the deposition of Aprígio himself, who claimed to have known that "Orlando and Carlos killed by ambush an old man known as Izídio" and "killed another man of unknown identity." His informant was Francisco da Costa Veloso. Francisco, however, in a deposition given on the same day to the same police chief, did not make any accusation whatever of Orlando or of Carlos.

Monday, August 21. Sister Nehida and I went to Lower Rio Maria to visit the base communities. Carlos asked for a ride. He was going to visit his parents and to organize some meetings. As we drove along the dirt road, we stirred up a dense cloud of dust.

We celebrated mass in the Carlos Drummond School, which is open on three sides. It has rough, improvised desks and a small blackboard hung from a crossbeam. The roof is thatched with palm branches.

At the end of mass, a couple came looking for me.

"Our daughter wants to get married," said the wife. "She is fifteen. Is it possible?"

"No," I said. "Only when she turns sixteen. It's a requirement of the diocese."

As we were speaking I noticed that the two young people looked disappointed. The father turned to them.

"You must get married in church," he said, "dressed in white. The important thing is virginity. Having a civil marriage first won't do, because then you can't come in dressed in white with a veil. Isn't that right, Father?"

The young girl, a pretty blonde, was staring at the floor. Her fiancé Raimundo, a twenty-three-year-old school teacher, was chewing his dark brown mustache.

"No," I answered. "Wearing white is not the most important thing. What matters is love. They should have time for their feelings to mature."

After mass, I went over to Jerônimo's house. His wife Delfina wanted to talk with me. We went out to the backyard and sat by the side of the brook. Her hands were shaking.

"Father, Jerônimo was free to marry. He was a widower. But I'm separated, living in sin. I lived with my first husband for seventeen years, and he left me for someone else. I've been living with Jerônimo for three years and we are happy. May I receive communion?"

While she was speaking I was thinking of Father Jaime Snoeck, a great friend from Juiz de Fora who taught ethics. He used to repeat a popular maxim: "Joined in faith is being married." He helped me to understand and reach out to persons who live in complex and difficult situations. Jesus did not expel the sinful woman from the banquet table.

Tuesday, August 22. At 11:30 A.M. we arrived in São José and stopped at the home of José and Maria, a couple from Goiás who live at the base of a ridge beside the little hut which serves as chapel and school. Maria was setting the table, around which were four wooden benches. She went to the charcoal stove and brought back pots of rice, beans and country-style stewed chicken. She also served *farinha puba* — a flour made of cassava soaked and fermented in water. Everything was simple and delicious.

After lunch people began arriving for mass. One of them was Lucidalva, the school teacher. She looks to be no more than twenty years old. She greeted everyone and disappeared into the kitchen. That's the way it is in the countryside. The men stay in the front room, the women in the kitchen.

Someone commented that married couples are separating a lot, and that it didn't used to be like that. One old man declared, "Times have not changed. It's just that people are more shameless."

Before mass Sister Nehida spoke with the community about models of church, illustrating with posters. One represented the church as a pyramid, with a rigid hierarchy. Another represented the church that dialogues, where everyone is heard and valued. Some people said they preferred the old way.

We later learned that this community is seriously divided. José and Maria fought to replace the teacher Raimundo with José's sister, Lindalva, alleging that Raimundo was not qualified to teach. Their actions created deep wounds.

Thursday, August 24. We set out early, on foot, for the Rainha da Paz community. When we reached the home of Dona Ilza and Seu João we were tired and hungry. Seu João brought us some pineapples from the backyard while his wife pounded rice with a mortar to serve us for lunch. She also served beans with the remains of a pork rib.

"The poor only eat tree fibers," said Seu João.

"This food is delicious," I said. "We don't need anything else."

Since they had not received our letter telling when we were coming, no one was here for mass. We took the opportunity to rest and to get to know the family better. They live with their children and with Seu João's older brother, who is deaf and mute. He communicates with gestures and smiles.

They are behind in clearing the land, as are most people around here, because of the rains. They will have trouble trying to get the burning done before planting.

Seu João told us about the problems the farmers have in marketing their crops. "The price of a sack of unhulled rice is twelve new cruzeiros (US $2.79), never more than that. But in Rio Maria, the owner of the machine that processes the rice sells it for seventeen new cruzeiros."

Sunday, August 27. We went to the Santa Luzia community where, besides celebrating mass, I had to do twenty-two baptisms. I got home exhausted. My body was demanding a cold beer.

7.

August 29 to September 20, 1989

A visit to the base community of Sete Barracos is the occasion for an introduction to a slightly eccentric French missionary and for Father Ricardo's recollection of past events related to the struggle for land in that region, including threats against him and false allegations in a major newspaper. He visits a farmer who talks about an attempt on his life, then returns to Rio Maria for the Parish Assembly of Base Communities.

Tuesday, August 29. Dona Paula, a short, thin French woman of seventy-five years, is dedicated to the gospel and to pastoral work with great passion, inexhaustible energy and a certain authoritarianism. She lives in a little cottage made of packed clay earth with a thatched roof, without running water or electricity, and travels the twenty-three hamlets in this area by bicycle or on foot. She helps the sick without charge from her domestic pharmacy, and, when needed, takes them to hospitals in larger cities. She argues with the mayor about the roads and gets involved in the running of the schools. She separates brawling drunkards, even taking knives from them, and dreams of transforming the region into a territory free from cane liquor, prostitutes and Pentecostals. She has defended with tooth and nail the rights of settlers against the large landholders, writing letters to congressmen, to governors and, during the military dictatorship, to generals.

This week I called Dona Paula to tell her that I was planning to visit the Sete Barracos community. She got right on her bicycle and traveled the thirty kilometers from Floresta to Sete Barracos in three hours. She was already waiting to speak to me when I got there at 10 A.M.

In her delightful French accent Dona Paula complained about how, for the past two months, they have been taking three truckloads of lumber out of Bela Vista every day. The small farmers have been surrendering the rights to the mahogany on their lots in exchange for the dubious road that the lumberyard constructs for moving the trees. What the lumber dealers

42

pay the farmers is a trifle compared to the profit that they reap in both the Brazilian and the international markets.

These farmers came to this area in the early 1980s, when the Bela Vista Ranch was practically abandoned. Three hundred families occupied the land, cleared fields, put up shacks, marked off their lots and began growing food. In 1987, after the farmers had been there long enough to have rights as *posseiros*, the rancher brought in police and hired gunmen to evict them. They burned houses, fields and granaries and tortured the men. That year the police held the area under siege for 132 days. A four-year-old child died because her relatives could not get her out for emergency medical attention after she cut her foot. A woman miscarried her first child. João Moreira de Souza, a married man with twelve children, accompanied two German reporters who were preparing an article about the land problem in Brazil for the magazine *GEO*. Fearing reprisal after the publication of the article, he fled from the area, crossed the Araguaia River and hid in Tocantins. He was hunted there and bludgeoned to death. Two days later, the gunmen killed another man inside Bela Vista and prevented his burial.

There were also threats against those who denounced the violence. Sister Rita, a German religious who works in Arapoema, learned about the torture at the ranch and went there to intercede for the victims. She was driven away and threatened with death. Gunmen went to Arapoema to kill her, but did not find her.

Right around this time, Minister of Justice Paulo Brossard set up a meeting of the Commission for the Defense of Human Rights at the City Hall in Conceição. Hundreds of people came, including widows, children and parents of farmers killed in the land struggle and other workers who had been shot or beaten. The place was full of police and the atmosphere was tense. The entourage from Brasília was late in arriving. When the Minister of Justice finally entered the hall, the people rose. Doctor Brossard took off his hat, set it on the table, and solemnly raised his arms in greeting to everyone present. The people responded in chorus:

"Justice! Justice! Land reform! Land reform!"

Doctor Brossard frowned in distaste and turned to speak with Romeu Tuma, head of the Federal Police. Then the minister and his whole retinue left, returning to Brasília without saying one word.

A journalist, looking as perplexed as I was, asked me, "What do you think of the minister leaving?"

"I didn't understand," I said. Then I added wryly: "He should have been satisfied, because the people cried out 'justice,' and he's the minister of justice. He should have been pleased, because the people cried out 'land reform,' and the government that he represents has made a lot of promises about land reform. Or is it that he agrees neither with justice nor with land reform? If he left out of fear of gunmen, despite the whole security scheme for protecting him, he should resign his position. Or is he afraid of unarmed people, of widows, or orphans, that the government that he represents does not manage to protect?"

The television networks did not present a single word or picture related to this incident. From that moment, however, the Araguaia Regional Radio, through one of its announcers, Sérgio Dias Guimarães, a lawyer for the ranchers, closed ranks against those of us connected with the Pastoral Land Commission and the Union of Rural Workers. Doctor Sérgio claimed that six people needed to be "eliminated," and he emphasized my name.

Around that time I received a phone call from the bishop of Tocantinópolis, Dom Aloísio Hilário, warning me that the four gunmen who had gone looking for Sister Rita were now after me. Although my life was spared that time, the scene still did not calm down. The newspaper, *Estado de São Paulo*, published on the front page the allegation that I had gone to Nicaragua and hired three Sandinistas to organize a guerrilla movement in the south of Pará, beginning at the Bela Vista Ranch. The reporter claimed as a source the district judge of Conceição do Araguaia. He also interviewed the president of the UDR, Ronaldo Caiado, who declared that I was "an extremely dangerous" person. He raised the suspicion that these guerrillas whom I supposedly hired had sabotaged a plane that crashed in the Carajás hills, killing Federal Minister Marcos Freire. Since the article was completely false, I threatened to take both the newspaper and Ronaldo Caiado to court.

Around this time Ernesto Cardenal, Nicaraguan priest, poet and government minister, visited Brazil. The press interviewed him with respect to these issues. He replied that the revolution was not being exported. What was being imported, on the other hand, was counterrevolution. The *Estado de São Paulo* published this statement, along with my denial of their previous report.

Wednesday, August 30. From Sete Barracos, I continued on foot to the home of Ubaldo, with one of his brothers as a guide. We crossed a river that was low and full of pools of mud and mercury. This mercury, which is used by the gold prospectors, is causing illnesses among people who drink the water and eat the fish from the rivers.

We finally reached Ubaldo's home. His wife served us rice, beans, chicken and cassava meal. During lunch I asked Ubaldo about an attempt on his life.

"There were four men wanting to kill me, because of my friendship with João Canuto. Not knowing that, I told one of them that I was going to town by bicycle and would be returning that same day. I ran into Zé the teacher, who suggested that we travel together. We took off, pedaling hard. At the top of the ridge we got off and pushed the bicycles. We passed a truck stopped by the side of the road and came to the fork between the new road and the old one. The men in the truck drove down the new one. I was feeling suspicious and said to Zé, "Take the old one." When the men saw that we were going by the other road, they fired shots above Zé, who was riding in front. We pedaled fast, like lightning, and survived."

The time for mass approached. After praising Ubaldo's wife for the food, we walked down a narrow path, crossing long trails through a forest with huge trees. We came to an open field, where there was a chapel with a thatched roof. Some people were already waiting for us. We practiced some hymns, out of tune, while we waited for the other people to arrive.

Friday, September 1. The Base Community Assembly began with lunch. There were twenty-eight representatives from various parts of this spread-out parish. A lot of people were not able to come because of the distance, scarce means of transportation and the high cost of the transportation that does exist.

Saturday, September 2. Today I received some upsetting news. Jerônimo's wife Delfina, with whom I was talking less than two weeks ago, was struck by a car yesterday in Xinguara and died. I went there to spend time with her relatives. Jerônimo is taking it very hard.

I returned to Rio Maria for the Base Community Assembly. I talked about the communities' mission and new way of being church, and about the relationship between this new way and the Bible. I used the book of Exodus and texts from the Gospel of Luke and the Acts of the Apostles.

In Exodus we read about the ordeal of Moses. He receives an order from God to enter into the process of struggle for the liberation of his people. Trembling, stammering, looking for excuses to flee from the call, Moses is like all of us at the moment of commitment. Our fears and fragilities take on flesh and threaten to suffocate us. But Moses conquers these weaknesses and accepts the charge, even if he has to learn to lead by trial and error. He learns that the Israelites do not need to accumulate goods (Exodus 16) or create situations that produce poor people (Deuteronomy 15). He learns from Jethro, his father-in-law, that power cannot be centralized but must be shared (Exodus 18). He sees that Yahweh is right with regard to the Pharaoh. Only by force would he let the people go free (Exodus 3). The difficulties of the journey of the communities are also recorded, when the people see the soldiers on one side of them and the sea on the other, when they use up their supply of food and water, or even when they feel nostalgia for their captivity in Egypt.

In the Gospel of Luke (4:18-19) we find Jesus explaining his mission — to bring the good news to the poor. He doesn't only make a preferential option for the poor, which today provokes so much controversy. He makes his option exclusive.

In the Acts of the Apostles the first communities were joined in an intense life of prayer and in the sharing of goods. They inspire us, even today, to develop a charity that is transformative, resolving the issue of the discrimination against and the dispossession of large numbers of people.

In Acts 3 we meet the apostles Peter and John on the way to the temple. They meet a man who has been crippled since birth and who asks them for alms. Peter says to him, "I have neither gold nor silver, but what I have I give you: In the name of Jesus Christ the Nazarene, get up and walk." The man got up on his own feet and went off leaping and praising God. No longer did he have to ask anyone for favors.

That reading reminded me of the farmers of Itaipavas, a small village in the municipal district of São Geraldo. There on the banks of the Araguaia lived Raimundo Fereira Lima—"Gringo"—along with other *posseiros* who had been thrown off the land. In June 1979, Bishop Hanrahan, who had been consecrated a little more than two months earlier, made his first pastoral visit to the parish. The people told their story to the bishop. They were a little unrealistic in their expectation that religious authorities would resolve everything for them. Bishop Hanrahan read this passage from the Acts of the Apostles to them. The farmers, on hearing the reading, understood that they had to walk with their own feet. They returned to the land. They were evicted again. They persisted and won the rights to the land.

Today Tonhão, who participated in the faith and politics course in Conceição do Araguaia, talked about Jesus in relation to the poor of his time. In the afternoon we listened to another speaker, whose theme was the history of exploitation. There were participants who did not agree, who insisted that wealth is merely the fruit of labor, and poverty of laziness.

I went to visit Dona Andrelina, who was in her hammock, suffering from intense illness, apparently of unknown cause.

"Sometimes," she murmured, "I spend the whole day without being able to see. I also feel pain in my hips. I have looked everywhere for help. In Goiânia a doctor advised me to go to a homeopath. My prayers are simple. The Lord Jesus listens to sinners, doesn't he, Father?"

I took her hands in mine.

Tuesday, September 19. Generally I travel with other people when visiting rural communities. This time I had to drive back alone. I had trouble crossing the Trairão bridge, which is long, uneven and composed of two planks on which you have to line up the tires. If you make one mistake you fall. I drove with extreme care, going slowly, stopping, looking, getting scared, trying to measure the width of the boards with my eyes. Then, right after getting through that ordeal, I got the jeep bogged down in sticky clay mud. Much to my relief a cowhand came by on a horse. He got a rope and tied the horse to the car. The car didn't budge.

"Don't be upset, Father," said the cowhand. "It must be the work of the devil."

Finally along came a pickup truck that was able to pull the jeep free. I went up and down hills, got stuck some more and was helped by prospectors who set aside their work to push the car. It took seven hours to travel 105 kilometers to the next community I was visiting. After celebrating mass I left quickly, in order to meet a commitment to another community that same night.

I didn't get there. I got stuck again and spent the night here on the road. So now I'm sitting alone, in the middle of this dense forest, worrying that, with all this wind and rain, some tree will fall on the car. It's ten o'clock in the morning. I've eaten nothing since breakfast yesterday. But I do have what is essential. There is plenty of water.

Wednesday, September 20. Yesterday I finally got the car out of the mud with the help of people who came by in a van.

• • •

Frei Betto helped to get me invited to the Third International Conference of Theologians, which will take place in Matanzas, Cuba. When the invitation came in July, I got together with representatives of the parish teams and asked them whether I should accept it. Everyone said I should.

8.

September 22 to November 2, 1989

Two young men figure prominently in this chapter: Neto, the young gunman who recently converted to the Assembly of God, and José Pereira, who escaped from forced labor on a nearby ranch.

Father Ricardo spends some time studying the causes of death in Rio Maria, discovering high rates of infant mortality and of violent deaths.

Friday, September 22. When I passed through the kitchen this morning Dona Maria told me about a near accident at the bus station.

"A soldier dropped a bag with a weapon inside. It fired. It could have hit a Christian!"

I smiled and answered, "It could have hit a non-Christian as well, Dona Maria."

She also had news from Xinguara. Several years ago the telephone company sold lines which, although paid for, were never installed. The buyers didn't receive any official explanation whatsoever. A single telephone office is not enough for a city of over sixty thousand people. Getting a call through is little short of a miracle. One has to join a long line of customers, suffer hours of waiting, and the call may not even connect. So the people of Xinguara lost patience. Dozens of angry men attacked the telephone office and looted it. Now people are saying that the same thing could happen in Rio Maria.

"They shouldn't destroy the station," said Dona Maria. "It's bad enough having to use it, but it would be worse not to have it at all."

Today is Dona Maria's birthday. Her friends are planning a surprise party in the parish hall.

Monday, September 25. Last week the judge conceded the *habeas corpus* requested in favor of Carlos and Orlando.

I heard a noise outside and opened the door. It was Expedito. I noticed

48

that he was looking a little apprehensive, so I asked, "What's new?"

"At the beginning of the month Pedro Paraná, the gunman, came looking for me. He has a lot of nerve. He said that he had received a proposal from a rancher who had bought land from Braguinha. The rancher wanted Pedro to remove the farmers that are living on it. I was uncomfortable, wondering where this conversation was going. Then the gunman told me that he was going to enter into an agreement with the rancher, and take his money, but then would seek out the farmers 'and help them win the land.' He had the gall to ask me to point them out to him."

Sunday, October 1. "They killed a man out front," a parishioner told me. "Just now."

I hurried outside. A crowd of young people were jostling one another in front of the Big Boy Dance Club. I saw the car from the morgue, with the body inside, beginning to move away. Two huge pools of blood stained the ground. The VW police car was parked in front of the house of Mayor Tião Aranha. Beside it were some soldiers, the police chief, the mayor and his wife.

"It was Neto," said a boy standing near me. "He got two bullets in the head. It had to happen." The boy was wearing a look of satisfaction and relief, as were several other people.

"If you feel threatened," said another boy, "you have to kill first. That's the law."

A thin, white man with an unshaven face approached.

"Where's the body?"

"Gone to the morgue."

"What? Don't they think that Neto had a family? They just carried him off like that? Where did the car go?"

I showed him the direction. He began walking away, but after taking a few steps turned back. "Was it a bullet?"

The witnesses were silent, perhaps afraid.

"Are you his father?" I asked.

"No. I'm his grandfather." He turned and walked away.

One of the boys shrugged and said, "Neto used to say that he would not die while his grandfather was alive. Well the grandfather never visited the families of Neto's victims. Now he has to live with the sorrow."

The mayor's wife took a bucket and a broom and began washing the blood from the sidewalk in front of her house.

Monday, October 2. Almost everyone in town seems to be in agreement in their satisfaction over the death of Neto. It's the topic of the day.

I went to visit Expedito, who wasn't feeling well. He told me that he was worried about the shooting in Braguinha's area. At Expedito's house I met Neto's sixteen-year-old brother, then crossed the street to attend the wake for a few minutes.

Wednesday, October 4. A fine layer of ash is covering the city and the sky, turning the sun red. The burnings have begun, over a month late because of the rain. Last year the fires spread from the fields to invade parts of the forests. This year there was practically no dry season, which worried the farmers. Because of the wetness the burning was only partial. The farmers cannot prepare their fields without fire. So they are complaining about the weather, the government and the ecologists.

"Those people who don't want us to be setting fires don't understand farm work," said João Martins, a fifty-six-year-old man with a round face and straight hair that is always falling over his forehead.

Another farmer was saying that Saint Peter must have signed President Sarney's decree. The government didn't want any burning and the saint sent all that rain.

Guaracy and Jean, agronomists who work with the CPT, have been trying to get the farmers to try new methods for clearing and fertilizing the land. It is not enough simply to prevent them from burning the fields. They need to be shown economical alternatives. IBAMA[1] has proven to be totally ineffective. It ignores the large-scale destruction by ranchers and harasses the farmers for their small fires.

Sunday, October 8. We are in the midst of the festival of Our Lady Aparecida, patron saint of our parish, with a heavy schedule of religious and social activities. The church has been full during the novena and the festivities. Dozens of people contributed their work and goods for an auction.

Thursday, October 12. Today is the feast day itself. We had the mass and the procession through the streets.

Friday, October 13. Roberto told me about a peon who escaped from slave labor. He's been in Rio Maria for thirty days, although Roberto found out only today. We went together to the house where he lives with his parents and brothers. His mother came to the door.

"This is Dona Rosa," said Roberto.

"People call me Rosa," she said as she extended her hand. "But my name is Maria Lucas Pereira Ferreira."

We sat down in plastic-covered armchairs.

"Dona Rosa is of the Assembly of God," Roberto told me.

She called José, her son. From the bedroom came a young man with a deformed face. His right cheek was swollen, making it difficult for him to open his eye.

"I was hired to work at the Espírito Santo Ranch, owned by Benedito

---

1. IBAMA is the government agency responsible for overseeing environmental protection in the Amazon — tr.

Mutran." José was speaking in a low voice and looking toward the door. "That was on September 5."

His mother interrupted. "It was his birthday. He went to that ranch without telling us. It was the first time that he went out like that. I've told him so often to be careful."

"The one who told me about the work was Seu João, owner of the Pires Hotel," José continued. "I went with fifteen others on a truck to the ranch. There I heard that they didn't pay and that they liked to kill. I got worried and began to think about escaping. I was clearing pasture land, working on a team with Zeca, Neguinho, Ceará and Paraná. On September 13 at 3 A.M. Paraná and I escaped. We went straight into the woods, through territory that we did not know. It was a long, hard trip. I was getting very hungry. At six o'clock that night we saw a road and decided to risk taking it. We walked for two more hours."

A strong wind pushed open the door, blowing dust and dry leaves into the house.

"At 8 P.M. we met up with four armed men. They turned their weapons on us. The foreman was with them and he said, 'You're running away!' Then he shot Paraná in the back of the head. Paraná fell down dead at my feet. They brought a pickup truck that they had hidden in the brush. They unfolded a large canvas tarpaulin in the back of the truck, threw Paraná inside and rolled him up. They ordered me to walk. I thought, they're going to shoot me. I lowered my head and put my hand up." José got up from the chair and showed how he had ducked and tried to shield his head. "The bullet went through my finger, entered my neck and came out below my eye, splitting my cheek bone. I fell on the ground and pretended to be dead. They rolled me up in the same tarpaulin as Paraná and left us in the back of the pickup. I heard them talking about what to do. One wanted to throw us in a river. They finally threw us out on the edge of the road, near the headquarters of the Brasil Verde Ranch. After they drove away I went and found one of the guards of the ranch. He brought me to his manager. The manager helped me, ordering a car to take me to a hospital in Xinguara."

Dona Rosa said that the hospitalization cost the family 960 new cruzeiros (US $96.50). The medicine cost another 700 new cruzeiros.

I asked José for Paraná's full name.

"I don't know. I never saw his documents, but I know that he was from Ourilândia. He was about twenty years old. His family doesn't know that he's dead."

José said that he had told the police in Xinguara where to find Paraná's body. The police said that they went there but didn't find it.

"What do you intend to do?" I asked.

José and Dona Rosa said that they did not know. They were obviously afraid.

"Dona Rosa," I said, "your son was saved by a few miracles. A bullet passed through his head and he didn't die. He pretended to be dead and the gunmen believed it. They were going to throw him in the river and changed their minds. They tossed him into the truck and he didn't get more injured than he already was. He went to a ranch, asked for help and got it. God protected José. Now he has a responsibility. José saved himself and maybe can save those who are still in that hell. He can't just abandon them."

I proposed that they go to Brasília, because the problem is under the jurisdiction of the Ministry of Justice and contact with the press is easier there. I offered to help them get there. Dona Rosa said that she would think about it and consult her husband.

Peon

I am a short-term laborer
captive in the freedom of the forests,
prisoner of long days,
with no local roots.
Boat without course,
story without history,
peon
on a short stretch of road,
on a short term of life.

Wednesday, October 25. Last night Dona Marcelina organized a procession. About fifty children and ten adults gathered in the light from a lamp post, carrying green branches and white flowers.

"The people are upset about all the violence and death," Dona Marcelina explained. "The green branches symbolize hope and the white flowers peace."

They read a long list of persons killed in this area.

Today I passed by the morgue, and stopped to talk with Vilmar, who works there, asking him about someone who had been shot.

"He didn't die. He's alive. I saved him without knowing that he was a thief. If I had known—"

"Don't you think you still should have saved him?"

"Maybe, but a lot of people criticized me. They said that I shouldn't have saved him because he's a bandit."

I went to the telephone station to wait for a call from Ary Franco, the editor of the Catholic newspaper *Opinião*. He had received information from Brasília about my report on slave labor on the Espírito Santo Ranch. He wanted to know whether there had been more news. I told him that last Wednesday José Pereira and his mother went to Belém, where they spoke with the Federal Police and with the press.

On my way back from the phone station I stopped again to talk with

Vilmar. I asked him what was the most common cause of death in the municipal district.

"Murder by stabbing."

"Are there a lot of deaths among children?" I asked.

"Only newborns."

"What do they die of?"

"Dysentery."

He invited me to see the reports. I found a huge number of forms spread out in no particular order. There isn't even a registry book, but only loose, dirty forms. I picked up one and saw that the cause of death was not noted.

Thursday, October 26. Two men about 50 years old and a 16-year-old girl came to my door. The better-dressed man asked for the priest.

"I am he," I responded.

"Look, Father, I went to the pastor of Xinguara, Father Pedro, to arrange for my wedding. He said that he would do it only if we had been courting for six months."

The young girl was the prospective bride. The other man was her father.

"Since you live in Xinguara, the priest that you have to speak with is Father Pedro."

"No, Father, we live in Rio Maria."

I called him into the office, leaving the father and daughter in the living room.

"You're married," I said, guessing, since we had never met before.

"Yes, but widowed. I have my wife's death certificate." He handed me the document.

"Your address is in Xinguara."

"That's because I have a house there."

I noted the date with surprise. His wife died two months ago.

"This death is recent. And you're already thinking of getting married? How long have you been courting this girl?"

"One month."

"Did you love your late wife?"

"Very much. I can't forget her."

"If you loved her so much, wouldn't it be better to wait a while to get married again? Do you love this girl?"

"No. My love is for my wife. There is no other like her. I will not love any other woman as much."

"If you don't love the girl, how can you marry her?"

"Well, who will clean my house? Who will wash my clothes? Who will cook my food? Who will take care of my children?"

"Do you want a wife or a maid?"

"I don't want a maid. They're too expensive."

I asked him to go back into the living room and I called the young girl. She came in looking timid. Her father was with her. I asked him to wait outside. He stood near the door. I insisted that he sit down in the other room. Then I went over to the stereo and put on a Wagner Tiso record.

"Where do you live?" I asked the young girl.

"In Xinguara," she replied.

"And your fiancé?"

"Also in Xinguara."

"Do you love him?"

"No."

"So why are you here?"

"My father made me do it."

I called the two men into the office and explained that there could be no marriage without full consent. The young girl looked relieved. The two men walked out with heavy steps.

> Little Missy becomes a young girl;
> Miss Young Girl becomes a woman.
> It's a sing-song by the riverside
> where there is a bird in a cage.

> One day the cage is opened,
> the bird rises in flight.
> And Missy the woman sighs
> in her desire to fly.

Saturday, October 28. Yesterday I spent a few hours at the registry studying the number of deaths recorded there and their causes. The owner of the registry is Doctor José Claudino, who has served as a lawyer for large landowners. He proudly showed me the furniture in the office, all of mahogany, and talked with enthusiasm about the furniture in his house in Conceição and in his apartment in Goiânia. Then he talked about one of the recent murders.

"You should have seen the cold indifference of the guys involved when they talked about the murder. They'll be freed, because they are first-time suspects. But they could be killed. If they had killed my father, I would do the same."

"Do you think that that's the solution?" I asked.

"I'm not Jesus. If someone strikes me on one cheek, I crush him."

"You're not Jesus," said one of the young women who works for him. "And you're going to have problems meeting Him."

"No way. I'll find an angle."

"I learned about this murder," I said. "But I also learned through a lawyer that the prisoners were tortured. Those who are tortured give questionable testimony. And those who got information from them know that they can get it that way again."

"I don't agree with torture," he replied. Then he changed the subject.

"I treat my employees well, and I pay them better than the majority of commercial houses."

As I went over the records I discovered that a large number of deaths were not registered, unless there were relatives of the victims who took an interest and paid the registry. For other deaths there is a doctor's certificate, which gets lost in the mess at the morgue, where there are hundreds of identification cards mixed in with the forms.

The registry began keeping records for Rio Maria in June 1988. Of the ninety-seven death records there were twenty-one cases of homicide, with seven in 1988 and fourteen in 1989. In 1988 there were five other deaths that could have been homicides and in 1989 seven of these. This ambiguity is because of certificates that are incomplete. They mention traumas, for example, without other information. There were seven registered for work accidents and eight for traffic accidents. So of the ninety-seven deaths, forty-eight were of violent causes. Only fifteen of the deceased were born in this state; of these, one was a child and thirteen were newborns.

Elvira

Death is an uneasy companion
that deeply touches us.
It invades, by night, the hovels of the poor.
It comes too soon,
invading our dreams.

Death is colored by doubt.
Yesterday I baptized Elvira,
a child of a year and a month,
skin and bones, disfigured face.
A thread of blood slowly seeped from her eyes
and spread over her lips, over her face.

With water, by the light of an oil wick,
I baptized her in the name of the Father
who wants us to be sisters and brothers;
of the Son
who died so that no one would die that way;
of the Spirit
who strengthens faith and resistance.

This morning at three o'clock
Elvira became an angel, a pink and white saint,
flower of the hinterlands in a coffin of the poor.
She left this agony
and left others in agony.

Her mother cries.
Her father is working in the mines,
not even knowing that she has died.

Monday, October 30. Yesterday the Federal Police arrested the manager of the Espírito Santo Ranch and one of his employees. They did not, however, find either the labor contractor or any workers. Neither did they locate Paraná's body.

Thursday, November 2. At 8 A.M. I celebrated mass for All Souls' Day under a tree in the old cemetery. A large number of people gathered around the table used as an altar. The cemetery had not been mowed but was in better condition than last year.

A little after we began an elderly gentleman put his hand on my shoulder and asked, "Father, whom should I vote for?"

"Look at the candidates and see which one better defends working people," I answered.

"But Father, I want to know who you think will help us most."

I explained to him that this was not the proper moment for such a conversation. I suggested that he visit me at home.

The 4 P.M. mass was in the new cemetery. There were a lot of people already at the graves. Flowers and candles were everywhere. In one corner, to the left, I heard the voices of women praying loudly. I approached them. There were three women on their knees, piously reciting the rosary. Two men accompanied them. I passed slowly among the hundreds of tombs, observing the social differences. Some graves were simply in the ground, sometimes with a rough cross at the head. I saw others with monuments of cement, or of finer material, with a photograph of the deceased surrounded by ceramic or plastic flowers. I went to the grave of João Canuto, where I found Carlos and his brother José Ricardo, lighting candles. Further down was Neto's grave.

We began the mass under a hot sun. Irá gave the commentaries, Rosimar led the hymns, and the readings were distributed among various persons. During the celebration we referred to the continuous list of premature and violent deaths. I used the data that I had gathered at the registry and the funeral parlor as part of my reflection.

9.

November 6 to November 24, 1989

Another trip to visit rural communities terminates at the home of Carlos Cabral's father, Seu Leandro, who shares his views and experiences on a variety of subjects, including land struggles, politics and the natural environment.

The campaign for the first democratically elected president in twenty-five years is in full swing. The winner in the first round of voting is Fernando Collor de Melo, the favored candidate of the right. The two main opposition candidates are Leonel Brizola, governor of Rio de Janeiro and a perennial Brazilian politician of the left-of-center, populist variety, and Luís Inácio da Silva ("Lula"), a former factory worker and strong labor leader.

Monday, November 6. At 10 A.M. Sister Lourdes and I left for the base community of São João in Lower Rio Maria. People in this area are happy because there is a new bus route through here. They are hoping that they will save money in the transporting of their farm products and of themselves. Owners of pickup trucks charge twelve new cruzeiros to transport each sack of rice, which is almost half of what the farmers get for it at the market.

"The bus will be cheaper. They'll charge five new cruzeiros for a passenger or a parcel."

Before continuing the trip we learned that before the next bridge there is a short stretch that is difficult to travel.

"It's as slippery as soap," someone told me, "because the river rises and floods it."

Wednesday, November 8. We found that those who had warned us about the road were right. The jeep got stuck before the bridge and we had to get help from some men to pull it out.

After lunch we headed for the Carlos Drummond School. On an

57

embankment just before it we came to the pickup truck belonging to Flori, who transports people out this way. It was stuck over a ravine, with two of its wheels hanging over the edge. We had to wait while thirteen men using levers improvised from pieces of tree trunks raised the pickup and pulled it back onto the road. Sister Lourdes went ahead on foot to talk with some of the people waiting at the school. When I got there they were practicing hymns.

Thursday, November 9. I was sitting inside the shack of Carlos Cabral's father, Seu Leandro, and looking out at the dogs and the hens in the yard. This shack is in a beautiful spot. A thread of water passes beside the house, curving and then emptying into the clear brook a few yards away. This water provides for the needs of the family and of the animals.

As people arrived they joined in a free-flowing conversation.

"When I left Goiás," said Seu Leandro, "I was angry because I couldn't get work. People were saying, 'If you don't like it you can leave.' I struggled a lot, but I never got into gold prospecting. Money in the hand of a prospector is like an itch on a monkey's bum." After his wife served us coffee he continued, "With threats from the ranchers, our lives were invaded by fear. One day I said to a rancher, 'You shouldn't talk about God, because I don't think men with a lot of money can believe in God. You rich people grabbed the best lands. You took the areas with all the hard wood. You get protection from the government. A rich man has only to say "Hey!" and the Federal Police come. Pushed by hunger, we left known places. We couldn't go back. The little people got the worst lands.' "

The conversation went on for hours. There was no lack of complaints about the new bus line. "It's more expensive than the pickup trucks!"

My body was crying for a bed. They set one up for me in the boys' room.

On Certain Nights

On certain nights
thoughts come thundering in on horseback
disturbing my rest.
A bright star
sheds its light before my eyes.
On some nights
I am a horseman.
Thoughts gallop ahead of me,
harassing me with ideas,
balancing me on the thread of reason
or encumbering me with feelings.

My eyes are lit with sparks of fire!

Friday, November 10. Light invaded the room early in the morning. Through slits between the sticks of wood that serve as a wall, the sun came in, chewing up the shadows like a glutton. I got out of bed and went to the stream to wash my face. The family was already up, the kettle was steaming on the tripod and the smell of brewed coffee filled the air.

"I love nature," Seu Leandro was saying, "but she needs to be taken care of. Nature needs the forest with all its birds and animals. I find the wildcat beautiful. The jaguar looks like a painted wildcat, only smaller. There is the *irará*, which is a small black cat with a long neck, round head and a white or yellow collar." Seu Leandro does not know the word *ecology*, but he is a dedicated ecologist. "I want to maintain this forest just as it is. The forest is virgin and I don't want to offend her."

Sunday, November 12. Collor's[1] supporters organized a big motorcade and a rally with dancing.

Two reporters from *Manchete* magazine have come from Rio de Janeiro to cover the elections in the south of Pará. They want to catch the atmosphere of the northern cities. I invited them to visit José Pereira, who just returned from Belém with his mother. He is looking better now that the swelling in his face has gone down. Dona Rosa told us about their trip to Belém and about the contacts they made with government authorities and with the press.

"We talked to the newspaper and television people. The newspapers didn't give us a thing, maybe because the owners of the papers are friends of the moneyed people in this region. But it did come out on television. The owners of the television stations live far from here and probably don't know the ranchers. I talked only with my back turned. I didn't want my face to appear on television. It's dangerous."

José, who had been listening in silence, spoke up. "I came back with the Federal Police from Belém. They found the car that we had been in. They also found the tarp with blood stains. The employees of the Espírito Santo Ranch said that it was pig's blood from an animal that they had killed. The gunmen fled, and the police didn't arrest anyone. Not even the manager. But I did sign a receipt for the manager. He paid me fifteen hundred new cruzeiros for the hospital expenses."

"And we spent more than three thousand!" exclaimed Dona Rosa. "The lawyer had told us to demand fifty thousand new cruzeiros (US $4,166), because the bullet injured José's finger, interfering with his ability to work and, besides, he'll need another operation on his face. He has to go back to Belém."

She showed us the receipt in which José waived the right to demand more from the ranch. He is a minor, however. I believe that lawyers will be able to contest the amount of the payment.

1. Right-wing presidential candidate — tr.

Monday, November 13. I took the journalists from *Manchete* to visit Carlos and Luzia. They live in a little house without indoor plumbing. Since Carlos knows that he could be shot at any moment, he takes precautions. He came in from the bathing area in the backyard wearing only a towel but carrying a rifle.

Thursday, November 16. I went to Conceição do Araguaia to vote. I can see the obstacles that the rural workers face in voting, because there are no polling places in the countryside. Getting around is difficult, if not impossible. There is transportation provided for those who promise to vote for specific candidates.

I voted in one of the schools in the Capelinha neighborhood, where there were a lot of people in line and the inspectors from the parties were near the voting boxes. Three young men stood out because of their better clothing. One was wearing a shirt with an ecological slogan, although I know that his family is destroying the rainforest. Another is the son of a former mayor of Conceição do Araguaia. He and the third one were campaigning for Ronaldo Caiado and defending the UDR. They decided to take a poll to find out who was voting for whom. When they came to me I anticipated the question.

"I'm voting for the candidate of the workers. For Lula."

"It figures," said the former mayor's son. "You look the PT type. Do you know that Lula accused my candidate of ordering the castration of a peon? Well, peons should be more than castrated. A squatter who invades the land of my family dies. Lula is a terrorist."

"A terrorist is one who provokes terror," I said. "Terrorism is what you are doing in this line. This is what you defend: the castration of a peon, the murder of a farmer, the return of the military. This is terrorism. Is that the only weapon that you and your candidate have?"

The ecologist took the subject in another direction.

"I don't know why there are still women who have the gall to run for office," he said in a loud voice. "I would never vote for a woman. Women don't have their own ideas."

He then made a lewd remark that caused some women, even those supporting the same candidate as he, to cry out in indignation.

Sunday, November 19. Most of the votes have been counted. Collor easily gained the majority. The struggle for the second place is between Brizola and Lula.

I met Eunice, the public prosecutor, at the children's mass. She is living in former mayor Laranjeira's house. This fact compromises her impartiality in the inquest investigating the death of João Canuto, since Laranjeira is one of those accused of intellectual authorship of the crime.[2]

2. The intellectual author of a crime is the person who suggests that it be committed—tr.

After evening mass I stood outside the church, watching the intense activity and hearing the noise of the various sound systems. Fourth Avenue, at this stretch, has a lot of bars, ice cream shops and even a dance hall, the Big Boy. At this hour there are hundreds of young people, dressed in their best clothes, flirting with one another as they pass by on foot, on motorcycles and in cars.

Monday, November 20. Lula will be running in the final election, but Brizola is furious and demanding a recount.

Friday, November 24. I've stopped in Rio de Janeiro on my way to Cuba, and am staying with my friends Cynthia and Adair. When I got here, late last night, Adair was talking on the telephone with Dom Mauro Morelli, bishop of an area on the periphery of Rio. He handed me the phone so that I could greet the bishop.

At 7:30 tonight the doorbell rang. In walked Gilberto Gil, Caetano Veloso, Jorge Mautner and Nélson Jacobina.[3] They had come to speak with Adair about preparing television spots for the Brazilian Popular Front. Caetano and Gil had supported Brizola in the first round and were considering supporting Lula in the second. Caetano confessed his apprehensions up front.

"I'm in sympathy with the PT, but a presidential campaign may be premature. The party is new. Isn't it blazing new trails? How can it govern without the support of congress?"

I remembered that in Araguaia we had the same concerns. Heloisa had been raising this kind of question.

"I have two hopes," I said. "One is based on reason and the other on sentiment. Living daily with the land problem, with the dramatic presence of death that reaches even my friends, I want changes urgently. However, in the rational sphere, I am afraid that haste could interfere with a long-range project."

Caetano raised questions about the best political model and about nationalism.

"This is not the time to worry about the question of the party, Caetano, but of the nation," said Adair. "The times demand change and offer an opportunity for it to happen. You, Chico Buarque, Wagner Tiso and Milton Nascimento are examples of qualitative leaps in popular music and poetry. Isn't it time to recognize the leap that the Brazilian people want to make?"

We all laughed.

"I understand," said Caetano. "Let's start planning our participation in the campaign broadcasts."

3. Performing artists who are well-known in Brazil — tr.

10.

November 28 to December 25, 1989

Father Ricardo travels to Cuba for the theological meeting. While there he renews old friendships, tries to learn of the reactions of Cubans to changes in Eastern Europe, takes in the local art scene and participates in a community work project. He is blissfully unaware of the repercussions of this trip that are occurring in Rio Maria.

Tuesday, November 28. I left for Cuba yesterday after lunch. We arrived in Havana in the middle of the night. Early this morning we traveled to Matanzas, the location of the Third International Meeting of Theologians. The theme is "Evangelization and Colonization: Present, Past and Future of Latin America and the Caribbean." There are about 130 people here, including delegates and guests, coming from almost every part of Latin America and the Caribbean. There are some Europeans and a significant presence of North Americans. I found some Brazilians who came for the meeting and three others who live in the seminary here.

I was interested in learning about the reactions of people in Cuba to *Perestroika* and recent events in Europe. In public pronouncements Fidel talks about the process of adjustment, but not of any hope of deeper transformations. During the intermission I went looking for Ana Maria and asked her how she saw the changes in Eastern Europe. She said that she interprets them as the result of a mistake, a mere return to the values of the capitalist world. I asked her if the resistance of the people to party directions and to the state is not a symptom of the errors in the models implanted. She scarcely acknowledged what I said. We didn't get to discuss this in greater detail because there were so many people at the meeting and so little time between activities.

Wednesday, November 29. Theologian Jorge Pixley from Nicaragua gave an interesting presentation. He commented on the characteristics of the Christian Latin American Popular Movement and elaborated on a new

62

reading of the Bible. It should be scholarly but without losing its connection to the people. Pixley talked about Micah and his denunciations of the large landowners and dominators of Jerusalem.

Among the other speakers that we heard were Raúl Vidales from Mexico, speaking on "Theology of the Empire"; Fernando Martinez on "Political Analysis of the Present Continental Situation"; and Valéria Rezende from Brazil on "The Specific Struggles of Women."

I was called to the phone. It was Alexei from Havana. We made plans to meet on Saturday.

Saturday, December 2. The meeting ended yesterday. It was interesting to see certain people again and to get to know others whose personal witness is being heroically developed on our continent; to learn first hand of the struggles in El Salvador, of the hopes of Nicaragua; to be with people who deepen the relationship between faith and politics in the flesh and immerse themselves in the passionate adventure of the construction of the Kingdom.

I had been waiting, however, for a word about the winds blowing in the Soviet Union and in socialist Europe. I had also been waiting for something about the repression of the students in Tiananmen Square in Peking. Finally the topic was touched upon, but not in a satisfactory manner. I was carrying with me the most recent issue of *Manchete*, which I had gotten shortly before leaving Brazil, and which contained an article about the fall of the Berlin Wall, with a lot of pictures. That generated enormous curiosity among the Cubans. What impressed me was the position of the people closest to the Party. They pretend that there are not any serious questions at stake. The gist of it is like this: The Communist Parties are right, and the population of these countries is completely manipulated and mistaken. They let themselves be deceived by imperialist propaganda. Regarding China? There were no deaths among the students. Soldiers, however, were attacked by young people and slaughtered.

At the end of the meeting we approved a type of credo, called the "Declaration of Matanzas III." Afterward I went to Havana, where I stayed with the Dominican priests and seminarians. This is the second time that they've put me up.

Today I talked on the phone with Marina, wife of Doctor Chomy Miyar, private secretary of Fidel. She invited me to participate in a collective work effort in the Nueva Vedado neighborhood tomorrow.

This afternoon I went with Alexei and Milena to the Third Biennial Art Exhibit of Havana. This couple breaks the Cuban patterns because they both behave in ways that are not very orthodox. Alexei is in love with Brazil, wears earrings, writes poetry and considers himself both Christian and Marxist. He is against the bureaucracy and the closed system. He wants access to books that are not available. Milena's family looks at him with suspicion because he is Christian. Milena has a tense relationship with

Alexei's family because they consider her somewhat of a hippie.

The bus dropped us near the Palace of Fine Arts. The exhibit had some interesting works. Eroticism is emerging in Cuban art and nudity is now permitted. In painting it is breaking out full force.

I wanted to buy a woodcut print. I was carefully choosing one when Alexei invited me to visit a friend of his who is a painter and who also produces woodcuts. We went into the beautiful old part of the city, with its big houses. I felt as though I were in Brazil. I looked at people's faces, saw their colors, and felt as though I had not left my own country. We went to Monserrate Street and climbed the stairway to the fifth floor apartment of Antônio Canet. The painter lives alone, surrounded by his works and those of other artists. He was very friendly. He served us tea and showed us his home and his works. Canet fought against Batista and worked beside Che. He is Christian, with a strong mystical accent.

He gave me three of his works.

Sunday, December 3. Marina came to get me early. In Nueva Vedado they've organized a collective effort to build an apartment building with one-, two- and three-bedroom units. When we got there Doctor Chomy was helping to raise a wall. He greeted me warmly, then taught me the art of applying cement and placing bricks. We worked intensively. When will we have something similar in Brazil? When will someone high in the political hierarchy, without visible political dividends, participate in collective work efforts?

Sunday, December 10. On my return from Cuba I passed through Rio, where I attended the show for the Brazilian Popular Front in the Sambadrome. The best musicians of the nation were on stage. Brizola was also there, as was Lula himself.

Saturday, December 16. Sister Lourdes and I spent the week traveling among the base communities in Araguaxim. On Monday we celebrated mass at São Sebastião II and on Tuesday at Our Lady Aparecida and São José. On Wednesday we visited Santo Antônio and São Cristóvão. To get to São Cristóvão we had to go part of the way on foot, because Sister Lourdes convinced me that we should not drive across one of the bridges, made only of three logs. Since it was raining and there was a lot of mud on the logs, the crossing was risky. We left the jeep parked by the side of the road, and we began the walk, after selecting what was strictly necessary, in order not to carry a lot of weight. Some stretches were especially slippery. I fell in the mud and Lourdes laughed at me. We then visited the communities of Cristo Redentor, Sagrado Coração, São Sebastião I and Banápolis. What a marathon!

Back in Rio Maria, I went to get a sack of rice processed at Seu José's rice machine. He waited on me solicitously. I asked about Dona Maria Ivo, his wife.

"She's in the kitchen," he said. "Why don't you go visit her?"

Dona Maria Ivo was cooking. She gave me a hearty hug. I complimented her on the renovations that they had done in the kitchen. She thanked me and hugged me again.

"I recently spoke ill of the priest and of the communists," she said with a smile as she continued hugging me.

"But what did the priest do wrong, Dona Maria?" I asked, surprised.

"I'm not going to tell you. You'll find out. The whole city is talking. But I'm your friend. I'll continue to be your friend. Let's not mix our friendship with political disagreements."

I left, wondering what had happened. Then several people came looking for me.

"Ricardo, Dona Maria Ivo got up on the truck during the Collor rally and gave a violent speech against you. It was twenty minutes of accusation. She said that you are Red and that hidden beneath your Bible is communism. She said that you transformed the church into a Committee of the Brazilian Popular Front. She also said that she was speaking as an insider, that she is of the church and everyone knows that. She was applauded!"

People were saying that I had gone to Cuba with money from the church festival, that I went to get economic resources for Lula and that I had taken a trip with Lula in a plane for who-knows-where. I decided to call a meeting of the finance committee of the parish and of the persons who were in any way involved in the talk about my trip to Cuba, including Fraga's wife Vânia. I personally invited her and Dona Maria Ivo. The meeting was set for a time that was convenient for everyone.

Tuesday, December 19. Last night everyone concerned met in the parish hall, except for Vânia and Dona Maria Ivo. In addition to the finance committee and the critics, Sisters Lourdes and Nehida, José Batista, João Martins, Brás the mechanic and Expedito's sister Isabel were there.

I explained that I wanted to hear the criticisms, and that I could only improve if I knew what had been said.

At first no one spoke. Then someone confirmed that stories about the improper use of festival funds were circulating around town. Irá spoke up.

"It is unfortunate that Vânia is not here," she said. "She stated that Brás saw Ricardo sending a check to the Brazilian Popular Front with money from the parish."

The blood rushed to Brás's face. "Where is this Dona Vânia? I barely know this lady. I never said that. I don't know where she got that nonsense."

I regained control of the meeting, saying that I had heard this and other accusations, including some about clandestine meetings with communists in the church.

"Never was there a single clandestine meeting in this parish," I said.

"Various members of the Communist Party participated in meetings about the Comprehensive Municipal Law, but these were always public. We invited all the organizations that wanted to discuss the subject. With regard to the use of the money, I want to share certain facts."

I presented the bank statement for the festival account and a letter signed by the manager and the assistant manager of the bank. These proved that the money had been deposited and that nothing had been withdrawn to date. We had not even taken out the 20 percent to go to the diocese or the 10 percent for the maintenance of the parish. If I had sent money from this account, how could the absence of withdrawals be explained?

Regarding the airfare, I luckily still had the letter from Frei Betto, on official stationery, asking that I obtain in Matanzas reimbursement for what I spent to buy the ticket, and the airline receipt in his name, so that he could render accounts to church people in Holland. What was I doing in Cuba? I showed them the folder and the papers from the meeting, all with the logo of the event. I showed them a letter from the Regional Committee of the Christian Conference for Peace in Latin America and the Caribbean, dated May 24. I asked them if they didn't remember that in July I had met with many of the persons present, spoken to them about this invitation, consulted them on the question of whether I should accept it or not, and that they all had agreed with the trip. They remembered.

I clarified my right to participate in politics, a right guaranteed by the Constitution, and to affiliate with any party, to go to a rally and even to talk about it. I stated that I had voted for Lula in the primary and would vote for him again. I voted for him because I know him and because I know the proposals of the Brazilian Popular Front. Despite these rights, however, I do not have a party affiliation and I had the common sense not to get up on political platforms, since people in this city tend not to distinguish the private citizen from the ecclesiastical structure.

This afternoon Vânia and her husband Fraga visited me. Vânia was wearing an enormous Collor button. She explained that she was very sorry about not being able to be present at last night's meeting, and that she had heard that I had been persecuted. She wiped away some tears. I said that I, too, was sorry about her absence. The meeting had been set for that day and time in consideration of everyone's commitments, including hers. She claimed that some unexpected visitors arrived and that, since she had not prepared any dinner, she was obliged to take them to a restaurant.

"You know, I'm very religious," she said. "Charismatic. I voted for Collor because I was inspired to do so by Jesus. After the primary I received a circular that Afif's wife sent to the prayer groups, informing us that her husband is of the Charismatic Movement, and asking for votes for him. If it had come before the fifteenth, I would have voted for him. But Jesus made the letter arrive later. So I was able to vote for Collor without any doubts."

Monday, December 25. There were not many people at last night's mass because it was raining. The countryside can be difficult to travel in the rain, and terrible road maintenance makes even main routes impassable.

Today, much to my surprise, Carlos Cabral appeared, all ready to paint my house as a Christmas present. He worked all day and will return tomorrow to finish the job.

11.

February 2 to April 20, 1990

*In the process of telling about a bible course in Banápolis,
Father Ricardo sketches some quaint aspects of rural life. On
his return to Rio Maria, he visits several widows of unionists, who
relate the stories of the assassinations of their husbands.*

*At the beginning of April, Brás António de Oliveira, the
mechanic who was a former director of the Union of Rural
Workers, is murdered, along with his young assistant. The sermon which Father Ricardo subsequently preaches on Palm
Sunday seems particularly courageous in the face of death
threats.*

Friday, February 2. People are saying that there was another shoot-
out at the Suaçuí Ranch and that several people died.

Sunday, February 11. José Batista, Sister Nehida, Sister Lourdes
and I arrived a few days ago in Banápolis to give a Bible course to people
from eight base communities. The course began with thirty-two participants
and ended with forty. There was a lot of interest and readiness to learn.
We looked at some passages in the books of Exodus, Amos and Matthew.
It was the first immersion of this group in holy scripture. Airton was with
us for part of the course. He enlivened the group with his presence and
with his guitar. He is getting ready to go to Belém, where he will begin
studies of philosophy and theology at the regional seminary.

Yesterday Sister Lourdes was upset. "I went to take a bath and my new
watch fell into the sewage ditch."

The situation became a source of jokes. Who was going to dive in to get
the watch? Today we had already forgotten about it when Dedé asked for
silence and had a child present a wrapped package to the nun, with great
solemnity. She opened it and found the watch. Dedé had gone poking
around inside the cesspool with a hunting knife.

During breaks we went swimming to relieve the mental fatigue. For the

68

farmers work with hatchets and hoes is less tiring than study. While we were bathing in the river, the men told their stories.

"Back in Minas Gerais," said José Belo, "I worked in a literacy program. Four of my students were very strait-laced spinsters. For the lessons we used a book that came from the government. I was supposed to spell the letters to show them how to form the words. One of the women insisted that I not use certain words, because she thought that they had impure meanings. When she would forbid something, I would have to obey."

Then it was Bento's turn. "A boy doesn't have any sense, right? I was really bad. One time a bunch of us had a party. When it was over we snuck away, looking for some mares."

In the rural areas, where sexual morality is rigid and courting couples have to control themselves, even adults sometimes have relations with animals.

"The owner of the house saw us going in their direction. He got suspicious, followed us and took our clothes. We had a good time with the horses, but we had to go home naked. We got terrible beatings. Do you think I learned? One night I was in that same area and got the urge. One mare was my favorite. I thought there was no one else around. Suddenly a young girl came by. She wanted to pass, but the mare and I were blocking the path. I didn't notice the girl until she said 'excuse me.' After that whenever I would see her I would die of embarrassment."

Friday, February 16. Bishop Hanrahan telephoned me. Someone from Amnesty International has been in touch with him and will call me next Wednesday.

Saturday, February 17. Last night, on their way back from Marabá, Guaracy, Heloisa and Aninha slept here. Aninha and Guaracy had been in Gogó da Onça and were disturbed by what they heard. This estate has been infamous since May 1985, when eighteen gunmen, including the Guedes brothers, invaded a house and attacked a thirteen-year-old girl. After raping her they burned her alive. This week Aninha and Guaracy talked with a farmer who keeps track of what he calls violent occurrences. He described various crimes to them, as well as the murder of one of the Guedes brothers, Manoel. He was about to kill a man, but the man's wife came up behind the gunman and killed him with an ax.

Friday, February 23. Conceição do Araguaia. The Diocesan Council has been meeting all week. This council brings together lay people who are involved in pastoral work, along with sisters, priests and the bishop. We meet three times a year to evaluate, plan and reflect on the paths of evangelization. There is also the Assembly of the People of God, which brings together lay people at the grassroots level. In these assemblies they define the pastoral priorities for the next two years.

The council chose Sister Lourdes, Míriam, Heloisa, Father Hilário and me for the faith and politics reflection group. We met at eight o'clock this morning to discuss what we thought about this subject.

"We should find ways for the relationship between faith and politics to permeate all pastoral activities," suggested Heloisa, "whether related to land issues, catechetics, Bible courses, the liturgy or the political education team itself. This should be a continuous process that is shared with the base communities."

While Heloisa was speaking, I got called away for a telephone call from State Representative Valdir Ganzer of the Workers' Party. He wanted authorization to nominate me as candidate for lieutenant governor on the Brazilian Popular Front slate, or possibly for governor. I was in a state of shock. I explained to Valdir that I'm not affiliated with any party and don't have any party ambitions. He said that there was a consensus with regard to my name. I still refused. When I shared the news with my friends at the faith and politics meeting, they supported my decision.

Wednesday, February 28. Sister Lucila prepared the ashes for today's mass. We are beginning Lent, the time of conversion.

> There is the time of refreshment
> when the heart is at peace.
> There is the time of peace and the time of war.
> Sometimes they become mixed and
> they are confused.
>
> I am a tempest on a gray afternoon,
> rain beating wildly, wind unloosed,
> a cry in the darkness, cutting streaks of lightning.
>
> I am the becalmed sea, a quiet conversation,
> affection without words,
> the gentleness of a cat on a sofa.
>
> I have a Love who loves me
> and what do I know?

Thursday, March 8. I learned from Father Pedro that the gunman who murdered Tena has escaped from jail.

Tuesday, March 13. Yesterday the faith and politics group gathered in Redenção at the home of Father Aristide.[1] We worked all morning. At

1. Father Aristide Camió is a French missionary who was imprisoned for two years under the military regime — tr.

noon we went to Father Chico's house for lunch. Since the Diocesan Catechetics Team is also meeting in this city, there were about twenty-five of us. Guaracy gave us information about the Father Josimo Pilgrimage, which will take place in Tocantinópolis on May 5 and 6. He also told us about the meeting in Belém in March of widows of rural workers killed over land issues.

Early today I went with Expedito to visit several widows and to invite them to the meeting. First we visited nineteen-year-old Cecília Alves da Rocha, who lives with her parents in Vila Nova, across from Roberto's house. Her husband Djaci had been occupying a lot in Vale da Serra for four months when one of his fellow *posseiros*, Antônio Medeiros, was shot and hospitalized in Xinguara. When it became necessary to move him to a larger hospital, Djaci and another farmer took their friend to the bus station. While they were trying to put him on the bus, they were attacked by two gunmen. Although Antônio managed to survive the additional injuries, Djaci and the other helper died.

The front of the house is a café, where bottles of wine and cane liquor vie for space on a wooden shelf. Cecília invited us to sit on the bar stools.

"I was five months pregnant with Fernanda and was working in the field when I got the news that Djaci had been killed."

Cecília showed us two photographs. In one of them Djaci was at the Serra Pelada mining camp. Behind him I could see an anthill of prospectors climbing and descending ravines. In the other picture his body was stretched out on a board, covered with blood.

I explained that some organizations were giving legal assistance to the widows of rural workers killed in the land struggle so that they could get economic support from the state. Cecília decided to go to the meeting in Belém when she learned that we were going to invite other women from the town.

We said good-bye and went to Dona Geraldina's house. We found her with Marciel, Paulo and Luzia. Orlando was in Goiânia, and Carlos was away prospecting for gold. José was also not in. Paulo, for whom his mother has special affection, is young, single and works in gold camps within the municipal district.

The boy decided to give me a lesson in prospector language.

"You never worked at prospecting, so you don't know the words that we use. The 'hoser' is someone who works with a short hose, which is also called a 'throat.' The 'gunman' is the guy who controls the jet of water against the side of the gully, cutting grooves in the ground with the water. Then there's the *catarino*. He combs through the rocks, using that big fork with the ten teeth."

After the lesson, we talked about the widows' meeting in Belém. Dona Geraldina accepted the invitation, but only if Luzia would accompany her.

"Do you have news of Carlos, Luzia?" I asked.

"He doesn't have any way of sending news. He's far away in an isolated place."

At eleven o'clock we went to visit Dona Albina, widow of Belchior Martins. With her were three of her children and a few grandchildren.

"Belchior was assassinated on March 2, 1982." Dona Albina reached for a photo album. Some of the photos are yellowed with time. She showed us her husband at their son's wedding.

"There was already an agreement at the Canto da Pedra Ranch when Valter Valente and two other gunmen went there to make trouble. The *posseiros* had to leave the land, but they could harvest the rice first. They needed a place to keep the rice, so they built a granary. Valter Valente accused my husband of building a house, and filled him with bullets." Dona Albina sadly leafed through the album, then put her finger on the photo of Belchior in the coffin. "The nurses said that they saw more than 140 shots in his body."

On the walls of the living room are pictures of the children and posters of performing artists. Near the door is an enormous picture of Pope John Paul II.

"I haven't seen you lately," I said.

"I've joined the Seventh Day Adventists. I needed help to face the difficulties."

Now with the murder of the prospector with whom she was living she is facing widowhood for a second time.

Dona Albina accepted the invitation to go to the meeting in Belém.

I went out again with Expedito at 3:30 in the afternoon. We went looking for Lígia, widow of Ceará. She was in front of her house, holding one of her children. We talked with her mother, who promised us that she would go with Lígia to the meeting.

Sisters Lourdes and Nehida went to Xinguara this afternoon to see Maria Rocha. She told them that she had recently learned that her husband's murderer had been arrested again.

Friday, March 16. Yesterday Collor assumed the presidency of the republic in the presence of various heads of state. Today the economic austerity measures of the new government took the country by surprise. After all the celebrating and fireworks by Collor's supporters, they have become more quiet. Some people are sick with worry.

Saturday, March 17. I was talking with a man who sells mercury to gold prospectors. I asked him how many kilos he sells each month.

"Generally around five hundred," he replied.

"And the price?" I asked.

"I sell to the retailers for 1,370 cruzeiros (US $25). They sell it to the prospectors for prices that vary from 1,750 to 2,000 cruzeiros."

I asked whether he didn't concern himself with the consequences of so much quicksilver being discharged into the rivers and small streams. He said that there are not any risks.

"Mercury is very heavy," he said. "It's heavier than water. So it sinks to the bottom and doesn't have any effect."

"That's not true," I argued. "It affects the fish, who eat the mercury in the river bed, and then harms the people who eat these fish."

Sunday, March 18. A lot of people are outraged because their bank accounts have been frozen[2]—people who had sold everything they had to live off the interest, or to buy a house or land, or to pay for medical treatment. Some wanted to remove their money before the bank holiday. The managers tried to humor the customers.

"Didn't you see the interview with the new economics minister?" they asked. "She said that her own money was affected."

Thursday, March 22. The March issue of the German magazine *Brasilien Initiative* came in the mail. It contains Günther's article and Expedito's poem, "Homage to Chico Mendes." Our poet was very happy to see his picture and his poem published in Germany.

Wednesday, April 4. I came here to Juiz de Fora to spend time with my father while he is recovering from surgery.

Today I received a phone call from Rio Maria with terrible news. Brás Antônio de Oliveira, the mechanic, and his shop assistant, Ronan Rafael Ventura, have been killed.

Saturday, April 7. Conceição do Araguaia. Guaracy told me about a peon who escaped from the Arizona Ranch in Redenção. The man who fled told the judge that other workers, including women and children, were being held there, that there were beatings, humiliating treatment and even killing. When the ranch owner learned of the escape and the report, he freed the others.

There are more reports of slave labor. Fourteen peons fled from the São Luís Ranch and went to the village of Floresta. The manager of the ranch, however, arranged for a Military Police corporal to arrest them. Dona Paula found out, called together the local Human Rights Committee and reported the incident to the mayor of Conceição do Araguaia. The mayor asked that the police and the peons go to the City Hall. The corporal got worried and freed the workers. The committee met again, this time with the fourteen of them. While they were talking, the ranch manager, the labor contractor and five gunmen arrived. They wanted to take the workers away by force. Dona Paula faced up to them. She warned them that she had already talked

2. One of the first measures of the "Collor Plan" for stabilizing the Brazilian economy was to freeze all savings accounts—tr.

with the mayor and he was waiting for them. The manager and his men left. An immediate concern is how to free the workers remaining on the ranch.

Sunday, April 8. Rio Maria. During mass today I preached about the Suffering Servant, humiliated and marginalized.

"The Lord is described, in Isaiah, as the part of Israel that is just and suffering. The Servant is also identified as Jesus, who delivers his life for us, and who wants to liberate the dispossessed and oppressed masses. He gives his life so that we may have life. It is time for us to clean up our Christian practice. The death of the two mechanics should disturb our consciences. To what point do we have some responsibility for the crimes that are committed in our city? To what point do we cooperate in some form of collusion, even by omission?"

As I was looking over the congregation I saw persons accused of direct involvement in murders. So I kept going.

"At what point do I decide a particular death?"

Some people walked out of the church.

Later João Martins came over to the parish house.

"The ranchers think only of their own low level of life," said João in his slow, country speech. "Never anything higher. Just now one of them asked me why I don't get away from this church business, since even the priest is being threatened. I told him that the most important thing in life is God. He said that the problem of the conflict began with you, because you order people to invade land. I disagreed. There have been land problems here for a long time. It is the obligation of the priest to do what Jesus teaches, to support the poor. On the day of the burial of Brás and Ronan, I heard a rancher saying, 'There was a meeting to decide the death of Brás. Ronan died because he was with him.' "

João is the brother-in-law of Jurandir, who is accused of involvement in the death of Canuto.

"Jurandir wants to kill me, because I told about his part. One time he came by at two o'clock in the morning. I got up. My daughter Solange, who was eight years old at the time, jumped out of bed. She grabbed me by the legs and cried, 'Daddy, don't open the door! Don't let Uncle kill you!' I told her to calm down, and I opened the door. Jurandir said, 'I came to call you to go to Marabá tomorrow.' I told him that I couldn't. He left. When they arrested him much later in Conceição do Araguaia, I visited him, and he told me that he had intended to kill me. He changed his mind because he owed me a lot of favors and because he felt bad for Solange."

"Do you have a weapon at home?" I asked.

"No, but God always protects me. One time Jurandir came looking for me, saying that Tião Ferreira wanted me to come to his house. I felt uneasy as I got into Jurandir's car.When we drove near the church the premonitions got stronger. So I told him that I forgot something at home, and I got out of the car. Later I went to see Tião Ferreira. He told me that he had not sent Jurandir for me."

Tuesday, April 10. A gunman accused Isai of going to the market for the farmers in Suaçuí and warned, "That's why Brás died."

I talked with Isai about the murder of the mechanics.

"As soon as I heard the news," he said, "I went to Babaçu Road to see the bodies. Ronan looked as though he had tried to get away. Beside the bodies there was a piece of green nylon rope. It looked new. I said to the sergeant, 'If I were doing the investigation, I would start with that rope.'"

Wednesday, April 11. I visited Dona Maria da Glória, Brás's widow. The door was open between the house and the repair shop.

"It was seven o'clock at night. A man wearing jeans and a black shirt came to the door, and our little son called, 'Dad, someone wants you!' Brás was eating supper and watching the news on television. The man came in and sat down. He said that his car had broken down twenty kilometers from town. My husband said that it was late and that he had sold our car; so he could not go at that hour. The man said that he would get a car. The stranger left. I got Brás's shirt and gave it to him. He got dressed and picked up his gun as a precaution. The man came back in a gray Gol. The driver was shorter, dark, with nappy hair, also wearing jeans and a black shirt. The man said to Brás, "Get your assistant so we can go."

"Did the assistant always go along?" I asked.

"Yes. They always went together. Brás called Ronan and he came right away, wearing shorts. He ran back home and got his shirt and a large knife and put it in the tool box. I said, 'Do you always put it in the box? If you need it, what are you going to do?' He told me not to worry. The men put the tool box into the trunk of the car. Brás and Ronan got into the back seat. The license plate of the Gol was yellow, from Goiânia. Later someone saw a white VW following it."

"Dona Glória, do you have any idea who was responsible?"

"No. It's dangerous to go after that information."

Holy Thursday, April 12. Yesterday in the main church we celebrated the sacrament of reconciliation, communal and individual.

Tonight we had the mass with the ceremony of the washing of the feet. Afterward groups began taking turns in vigil before the Blessed Sacrament. Tomorrow at 3 P.M. we will have the way of the cross, followed by the adoration of the Crucified Lord.

Saturday, April 14. "Two months ago," said Expedito, "a small, dark man came looking for me, asking, 'How do you join the union?' I explained that he had to be a farmer and to have lived within the municipal district for at least one year. He said that the information was for his uncle, who had been in a union in Maranhão. I said that he could transfer his membership. When he left I was feeling suspicious. Three days later he came back and asked how he could buy land in Suaçuí. I told him that I had only a hundred acres and couldn't sell him any. About twenty days later Brás told me that he felt suspicious about a man who came to his garage twice. He described him. I told him that the same man had come looking for me and that I thought he might be a hired killer from the Suaçuí Ranch. Canuto's nephew told me that he was also walking around Vila Nova. He went to the home of Dona Geraldina, looking for one of her sons. I discovered some other things. On April 3, the day of the murders, four strangers were drinking in José Angelinho's bar, near the bus station. Three dark men and one white one. José Angelinho felt afraid. He thought that they might be police. They drank until night, then went to the Mineiro Hotel. After that, he saw two of them get into a white Gol and go in the direction of Brás's house. He didn't know what the other two did. They might have gotten into a light blue VW. On the same day two unknown men were hanging around near the home of João Martins, near the bamboo bush. One of them spread out a sheepskin and lay down under the bush. The other one stood there as though he were waiting for a car. They told people that they were going to catch the bus. One of Aprígio's kids said in a loud voice, 'You two work at Braguinha's ranch.' We know that Aprígio is a gunman on that ranch and that he was involved in the arrest of Carlos and Orlando."

It looked like it was going to be a long conversation. Expedito had a lot of information, the pieces of a puzzle — discovering the links, weaving the relationships, checking the facts, composing the logic of this violence, its authors. This is supposed to be the task of the police and of the judicial powers. Unfortunately, we cannot hope for much from them, unless there are strong pressures.

"Roberto, old Doza and I went to see Police Chief Pedro Vieira to find out more," said Expedito. "He believes that the main suspects are the gunmen from Suaçuí. He probably knows a lot of things, but he is as slow as a turtle to reveal them."

Friday, April 20. Nivaldo from the Pastoral Land Commission told me about his trip to Santana do Araguaia.

"I went to two ranches belonging to companies from São Paulo. In one the manager is a friend of the local pastor, goes to mass with his wife, praises Dom Pedro Casaldáliga and allows people to enter and leave the property. At the other ranch they very carefully guard the entry and exit of people. We were there last month to check things out. We found a shabby hut in which there were thirty men sick with malaria. I asked, 'Why don't you go home and get treatment?' Someone answered, 'Because we are in debt to the foreman.' Then I saw a man with a gun in one of the hammocks, and I realized that this was slave labor."

Unfortunately Nivaldo did not manage to find out where the peons were from or what their names were. If we knew in what city they were hired, we could find their relatives, learn their names, put together a report and have a better chance of freeing them. I suggested to Nivaldo that he go back there and try to get more information.

Father Aristide believes that the best way to put the brakes on the use of slave labor is to require the expropriation of the property, by the means provided in the Federal Constitution, which demands "the observance of the mechanisms that regulate the relations of labor." Since the law has been broken, the land is susceptible to expropriation. For this reason we are thinking of taking some of the peons who worked on the Arizona Ranch to Brasília to report the abuses.

12.

April 22 to April 24, 1990

The sons of João Canuto are kidnapped.

Sunday, April 22. I celebrated mass in Vila Nova. Dona Francisca lovingly prepared a table in her living room, set up chairs and invited the people of the community. The candles were lit, the flowers were arranged and the singing began. With the bread and wine, body and blood of the Lord, before my eyes I prayed for the dead. I prayed especially for João Canuto, who had lived for so many years in that neighborhood and had died so violently. Later I celebrated another mass in the main church. Shortly afterward Marciel Canuto, his sister Luzia and Roberto Neto came into the parish house.

"We have very serious news," said Roberto. "A Gol with four men inside stopped in front of José Canuto's house. The men went in, introduced themselves as Federal Police and arrested José, Paulo and Orlando. We went to talk with the police chief. He doesn't know anything about it. He claims that he can't help us, because he has no car and no telephone. We went to the mayor's house. He wasn't in."

"When did this happen?"

"A half-hour ago."

I looked at the clock: 9 P.M. I was so afraid of what might have happened to Canuto's three sons. We had to act quickly. To whom could we turn?

"Let's go talk to the judge and to the public prosecutor," I suggested, doubting even as I spoke that this would help any.

I didn't have the jeep. The sisters had taken it to Marabá, where they were participating in a walk in memory of Sister Adelaide Molinari. We borrowed a car and drove to the house of the judge. His car was in the garage and there was a light on in the living room. No one answered the door. We finally gave up and went to the house of Adilson Laranjeira, since that was where the prosecutor was staying. We stopped in front of a high wall, with a strong gate. Huge dogs were free in the yard, barking loudly.

We pressed the bell and, soon after, the former mayor opened the gate. He asked pardon for being caught without a shirt, then took us into the living room.

"The visit is short, Laranjeira," I said. "We need to talk with the prosecutor. Three of Luzia's brothers were just kidnapped."

"Doctor Eunice has gone to Belém," he said. "She is no longer staying here, but at the Hotel Mogno."

Before we could say anything else, he went off into another room. I had seen the prosecutor at the children's mass this morning. Now Laranjeira was taking too long. We were all tense. We were losing time! Unable to stand it any longer, I went into the room where Laranjeira was. He was talking on the telephone to Vice-Mayor Messias Peixote.

"The case is serious, Messias. The priest is here." He handed me the receiver.

"Urgent action is needed," I said.

"But what can we do?" asked the vice-mayor.

"Please call the police in Redenção and Xinguara. They have to block the roads, inspect the cars that go by."

I hung up the phone and we took our leave of Laranjeira, who said to me, "Father, why don't you ask for two soldiers to walk with you?" I didn't answer. He added, "In this city no one is safe any more."

On reaching the outside door, we saw the dogs and hesitated, afraid. Laranjeira moved ahead and held one of them. He ordered the other one to back off, and we were able to leave.

We went to the Hotel Mogno and found that Doctor Eunice, the prosecutor, had not in fact gone to Belém. She received us and sent for the police chief. Meanwhile I went to Vila Nova to try to get more details. The people were afraid and were not providing any new information. I returned to the hotel.

Sister Lourdes pulled up in the jeep. She looked tired from the trip from Marabá and bewildered by the news.

Roberto rented a car and went with Carlos's brother José Ricardo to Xinguara, while we drove Luzia back to Vila Nova. We found people in the street, despite the hour.

Someone approached and said, "I saw the car. It was dark, so I can't be sure about the color. It was gray or dark blue."

Lourdes and I got out of the jeep. A young man crouching against the wall of one of the houses spoke up.

"I saw the bandits' car going up and down the street all day. They must have used up two tanks of gas. There were five men. Two were wearing Federal Police vests."

It was eleven o'clock at night. If they were really Federal Police, maybe the three Canutos would still be alive.

Flesh

I am unraveling flesh in flesh
I am unraveling thread by thread
I am coming unraveled,
I am becoming shredded,
I am slipping away
at the point of a switchblade
the edge of the knife
the knife without end
I rely on men
who look straight ahead.

Painful stories
of blood
parade before me
undoing vain hopes
I unravel the flesh with the edge
I unravel the thread in the flesh
in the radiant morning
I fly above.

Monday, April 23. I was still awake at three o'clock this morning, thinking about the fate of the three brothers and feeling fearful. I dozed until 5:30, took a shower and shaved. At 6:30 the telephone rang.

"Father Ricardo." I recognized the voice of Dona Irene. "My Uncle Rafael just came from Xinguara and brought news of a young man who was shot. Can you come here?"

I got over there quickly. She was waiting for me at her front gate. Her uncle was sitting in the living room, looking nervous.

"I found Orlando shot," said Seu Rafael. "I met him at the Sapucaia gas station. He didn't know whether his brothers were still alive."

"How many kilometers is that from Xinguara?"

"Thirty."

"I'm going to speak with his family and then go to Sapucaia," I said.

"Isn't it dangerous?" asked Seu Rafael.

"Yes."

"Before you leave, stop by here and I'll go, too."

I went out to find Luzia and Roberto, stopping at the São Miguel station for gas. Then I went to the command of the Military Police and talked with a sergeant. He said to come back a little later, because he and a soldier were the only ones there. I was driving by the mayor's house when I saw Luzia, Marciel, Roberto and José Ricardo. I told them about Orlando's message. They went to get an ambulance while I went back to the sergeant. Time was passing, and we still hadn't left town.

"Sergeant, the mayor has already authorized an ambulance," I said. "We need to leave right away. How about if just you and the soldier come?"

He agreed and we left. We stopped in Xinguara to pick up Father Pedro, then headed north. In Sapucaia we went into the gas station. It was there that Orlando was hiding, according to the explanation of Seu Rafael. It was only then that I remembered that I should have gone to Irene's house to get her uncle, but Seu Rafael was already at the station.

"He has been taken to Xinguara," he said. "The city councilor José Bamburrado came and took him there."

"Is the injury serious?" Luzia asked.

"Yes."

She cried.

"Orlando is being taken care of," I said to her. "We have to worry about the other two." I asked those who were at the counter in the bar, "Do you know where the other two brothers are? Did Orlando say?"

"He said that the shots were fired at the entrance to the Rio Vermelho Ranch, at the crossroad of Pontão. Eleven kilometers from here."

The sergeant who had come with us was in no hurry. He was in the front seat of the car, drinking coffee. In the back were Luzia, Zé Ricardo and the soldier. We waited impatiently for him to finish his coffee. Then we drove off. Along the way I voiced criticisms of the complicitous actions of the police in relation to the crime. The sergeant looked indifferent, which only increased my anger against this government that doesn't investigate anything, that doesn't punish anything. We would soon be at the place of the shooting. Through the rear view mirror I saw Luzia's face.

"Luzia, you have to prepare yourself for the worst," I said.

As we approached the crossroads we saw two soldiers of the Military Police. We stopped the car and asked for the two brothers.

"The bodies are over there, near the peanut plants, beside the fence" — he gestured with his hand — "on the right side."

As we pulled up near where the bodies were, I noticed that Luzia was crying again. I turned and put my hands over hers, trying to comfort her. She calmed down and said that she wanted to see her brothers. We got out of the car. We saw the two bodies stretched out near the fence. The soldiers were searching the ground for bullets. There was a lot of blood by the edge of the road. There was a rubber thong sandal two yards away from the young men. I saw Paulo, the nineteen-year-old, lying face down at right angle to the road, wearing shorts. José had been tossed parallel to the road, up against the fence, his left arm bent, covering his chest, his dark eyes open and his pale face bathed by the sun, showing in the network of blood the path of the bullets. On the left side of his groin there were signs of blood and the fabric of his slacks was perforated. As I looked at his face I felt torn with grief, and I found myself thinking of pictures used in processions of our Lord's passion and death. I was also remembering the famous photos of Che Guevara when he died. Paulo's sparse beard framed his thin face. The sight of his frozen eyes, the abundant blood, the marks of shackles on his wrists, where the flesh was cut down to the bones, was so upsetting. We were all speechless. Luzia was sobbing. One of the soldiers kept saying that she should not have come. No one paid any attention to him. The police explained to us that, before we could take the bodies, pictures had to be taken. We asked the ambulance driver to go to Sapucaia and bring back a photographer, then left for Xinguara to check on Orlando. On the way we saw a car coming in the opposite direction. The driver signalled for us to stop. It was the car from the Rio Maria City Hall, carrying the Socialist city councilor Sebastião Vieira. He had learned what had happened and wanted to come with us.

When we got to Xinguara, we went to the mayor.

"The boy is in my hospital and is not in danger," Dr. Atil said. "The shot in his abdomen did not affect any vital organ. The most serious problem is with his arm, but that is already under treatment. As a security measure, I got a soldier to stay with him. This was related to the conflict at the Suaçuí Ranch."

"But you must increase security," I insisted. "A single soldier is not enough in this situation."

The mayor did not answer. We went to the Santa Luzia hospital. I found it strange that we were able to get in so easily. We passed through a corridor and turned right. At the end of this second corridor, on the left side, we found Orlando. I was the first one in. When he saw me, he smiled and grasped my hands tightly. I felt so happy to see his face and to know that he really was alive.

"You've been born again!" I said, laughing.

"I've been born again," he repeated. "I'm alive." His sister came into the room and they held hands. She started crying again. Orlando's face was red with emotion. Tears almost came to his eyes, but he held them back. Later he told a friend that he could not express the enormous sorrow that he was feeling.

The room was filled with police, the people who had been in the car from the Rio Maria City Hall, Father Pedro and the others who had come with me. One of the nurses became nervous and asked that only the priest and someone from the family remain. I sat down beside Orlando. He had two bandages, one over his abdomen and the other on his right arm. He was complaining about the pain.

"So what happened?" I asked.

"They came to the house and said that they were from the Federal Police. They arrested us. They put handcuffs on me, with my hands behind. Paulo and José were handcuffed together. They pushed me into the car, then my brothers. They said that we were going to Marabá. During the trip they were asking, 'How many have you killed?' We answered, 'None.' They asked if we were part of the invasion near Redenção. They meant Suaçuí. We said no. 'Yes, you are,' they were saying. I told them that I had already been arrested on that charge and that I proved in court that I had nothing to do with it. Then they asked, 'Do you know about the death of Brás, the mechanic?' We lied, saying that we didn't know. They didn't believe us. Then they said that it was the Federal Police who killed him. So I knew these men had killed Brás, because they said they were Federal Police. They were the ones. They said they were going to get Expedito and Carlos, but nothing would happen to us. They were carrying a machine gun, a 7.65, and three thirty-eights. We left Rio Maria and passed through Xinguara. Before Sapucaia the car got stuck. A wheel slipped between two planks of the bridge. They put me outside and forced my brothers, who each had one hand free of the handcuffs, to lift and push the Gol."

I asked about the color of the Gol.

"Gray. It looked gray. On a night without a moon, it's hard to tell. We continued on the road. We passed through Sapucaia. When we were near the entrance of the Pontão Ranch, one of them said, 'Let's go in here to piss.' I knew that they were going to kill us, then and there. They got out of the car and pulled out my brothers. I was the last one out. They hit me hard on the head."

"Was the blow with a gun?" I wanted to know.

"No, with a hand. Then the driver shot me. The bullet passed through my belly and hit my wrist. At that moment I did not even feel pain. I threw myself against him and against the other one who was getting ready to shoot me. I ran across the road and bumped into the wire of a fence. I fell over the fence, into the pasture. The bullets passed above me. If I hadn't fallen, I would have been shot. I got up and escaped through the pasture. I could hear the shots going off behind, beside and in front of me. I ran some thirty yards and landed on the ground. I got up, ran a little more and fell down again. It's hard to get up when your hands are tied behind your back. I stayed very still in the grass. Not moving at all. I heard a lot of shots. Two of the men were coming through the fence looking for me. But they closed the circle in the wrong place, leaving me outside of it. I noticed the brushwood just ahead of me. If I reach the brushwood, I thought, they won't get me. I ran into the old brush. It's almost forest. I heard them start the engine of the car and leave. I stayed in the woods a long time. I was afraid they were going to come back again. At 11:30 I went to a house near the crossroad. I asked someone to go to the road and get a ride for me, because I couldn't raise my arms. They were tied behind my back. The people were scared, so they wouldn't do it. But they offered to cut the chain, freeing my hands. It was midnight. I went out on foot in the direction of Xinguara, through the woods, afraid that the men would catch me. I was thirsty but afraid to drink, in case I might hemorrhage. At three in the morning I got to Sapucaia, where I hid."

Before leaving I said, "Orlando, they're not offering much security here. Wouldn't it be better to go to another city? Maybe Belém? Or would you prefer Goiânia?"

"Goiânia is better, because my wife is there."

"I'm going to Brasília on Tuesday. If you want to go to Goiânia, we can go together."

Father Pedro brought him clothes—shirts, slacks and undershorts. While we were talking the ambulance arrived with the bodies. We went out to arrange for the coffins and the burial and to telephone Belém and Conceição do Araguaia. Orlando asked José Ricardo, Carlos's brother, to stay with him. We all agreed on that immediately. A soldier, however, said no, because it was dangerous. I objected.

"He'll stay," I said. "He's a relative and Orlando needs him. With José Ricardo here he'll be safer."

The soldier didn't say anything. We returned to Rio Maria and José Ricardo stayed. We first stopped by my house, so that I could telephone Jerônimo at the Pastoral Land Commission in Belém. I asked him to pass the information on to organizations concerned with issues of democracy and human rights, and to send a fax to the secretary of public safety and to the minister of justice, demanding action. While I was on the phone, Police Chief Pedro Vieira came into the living room. I interrupted the conversation to ask what he wanted. He asked for the names of the victims. Luzia gave him the information while I continued with my phone call. The chief wrote down the information and interrupted me again.

"Did Orlando make reference to the Suaçuí Ranch?"

"Yes. He believes that the owners of the ranch are behind these deaths."

Sister Lourdes, old Doza and other friends helped to wash the bodies in the public hospital.

I got telephone calls from Belém, telling me that there would be two planes coming with a delegation, including state representatives Valdir Ganzer and Raimundo Marques of the Workers' Party, Councilor Socorro and Neuton Miranda of the Communist Party and Ronaldo Barata and Antônio Fonteles of the Socialist Party. They were planning to take Orlando to Belém.

Dona Geraldina came in from Canaan in tears, inconsolable. Roberto went with me to her house in Vila Nova. Shortly afterward Doctor Eurico came and sedated her.

The burial was set for 6 P.M., after mass. I received more calls from Belém, asking that we wait for the delegation.

> A bird of iron alights upon
> my eyes in silence
> it has red wings
> and a sad song
> suddenly there flow from me
> streams that tumble down
> to an ocean of sorrow
> the war without end has begun

Tuesday, April 24. Yesterday the people were waiting in the church from 5 P.M. I was fearful about the long delay of the politicians' planes. Burying the men without light was not a good idea. We would all become easy targets for bullets.

I received a message from Isai. A man called his house asking him to warn me to be careful. He didn't want to identify himself, but he said he was my friend.

The bodies arrived on schedule. Children and adults congregated and were obliged to form a line, so that everyone could get to the coffins. Later we began the religious ceremony. During the homily I talked about the time of justice in which we are not living, the time of peace that has not yet arrived. I commented on the murders of the two brothers and recalled those of Brás and Ronan and the tragedy that is falling on the homes of this city.

"There is a growing and continuous spiral of violence. Paulo and José are the recent victims, ambushed by the creators of sorrow, violence and death."

I reminded the authorities of their obligations to see that justice is done. I mentioned the enormous, terrible procession of crimes that have shaken this region. Although there have been repercussions throughout the country and even outside the country, these crimes remain unpunished. The logic with which we have been coexisting is that of terror, of the fastest trigger. The law that rules, that determines, is that of force, not that of right.

As I was speaking the delegation from the capital was coming into the church, creating some commotion. Dona Geraldina and Luzia were seated between the coffins. The mother, seated closer to Paulo, was caressing her dead son's face.

It was dark when we went out to the cemetery. At the grave side, before the bodies were lowered, there were speeches. Doctor Antônio Fonteles spoke with emotion. He recalled the death of his own brother and demanded that the municipal authorities investigate these murders. The mayor and some middle-class people, who were standing some distance away, left at that point.

Today the planes loaned by the state government took off, carrying, along with the delegation, Orlando, who had decided to be treated in Belém.

13.

April 25 to May 1, 1990

Right after the funeral of José and Paulo, Father Ricardo goes to Brasília to meet with the minister of justice and with the attorney general, and then to São Paulo for a Faith and Politics meeting. On May 1 he attends some Workers' Day Activities, including a special mass, and also spends time with Lula.

Wednesday, April 25. The sun was barely up when Guaracy and I left for Conceição do Araguaia. We stopped in Redenção to visit Father Aristide Camió, who gave me a large folder containing documents that would be useful at the meetings in Brasília. He contacted the federal attorney general and the minister of justice to make appointments. Two peons who had escaped from the Arizona Ranch would meet me there.

I landed in Brasília late Tuesday afternoon. My journalist friend Memélia Moreira was waiting for me, accompanied by two other journalists from Switzerland. We had asked that appointments be made for the next day, but Memélia informed me that Justice Minister Bernardo Cabral was already waiting for us. We had only a half hour.

"But Memélia!" I objected. "How can we find the peons who are coming for the audience and get them to the ministry with so little time?"

"I thought they were coming with you," she said.

"No, they came ahead. They are staying at CONTAG."[1]

"I'll telephone there. Meanwhile, see if you can change into more decent clothes."

"But I thought these clothes were just fine!"

We hurried to the ministry without having found any sign of the peons. Congressman Edmilson was already waiting for us. Shortly afterward other members of congress arrived. There were fourteen in all. The minister received them with enthusiasm. He said that it would have been a joy to

1. CONTAG is the National Federation of Agricultural Workers.

receive these "most important leaders of the left" had it not been such a grave reason that had brought them.

I described to the minister the overall picture of violence in the region. I talked about the murders of Brás, Ronan, José and Paulo, and also about the assassination of João Canuto, the investigation into which was still not concluded. I reported that since May 1980, when Gringo died, the large landowners had killed more than 170 persons in seven municipal districts in the south of Pará. I told him about the slave labor at the São Luís Ranch in Conceição do Araguaia, and at the Arizona Ranch in Redenção. I showed photographs, including those from national and international magazines that published names and pictures of the gunmen. They are known, and there is a scandalous neglect by public authority in the administration of justice. I told him about the urgency of ameliorative measures, which would involve the opening of serious investigations and the punishment of those responsible for the crimes. I alerted him to the need for quick action to liberate those being held captive at the São Luís Ranch. Minister Cabral promised that the Federal Police would act.

"Are you being threatened?" he asked me.

"There are others more threatened. Expedito, president of the union, Carlos, secretary of the union, Orlando—"

"The Federal Police can enter only if you say that you are threatened and that you don't trust the local police."

"I don't trust them. If you need me to confirm the threats and declare that I don't trust the state government, I confirm that."

"The Federal Police will act immediately."

"Minister, what does the action of the Federal Police involve?"

"You will have their protection. It is necessary, however, that you inform the police of your movements. Otherwise, it would be useless."

"But Minister, I don't want special privileges. Expedito, Carlos, the farmers are more threatened than I am."

"They will have protection."

He took the documents that I had brought, wrote something on a sheet and delivered the paper to Cabinet Chief Inocêncio Mártires Coelho.

Doctor Bernardo Cabral reminded us that he had commitments to Human Rights and that he had been president of the OAB.[2] Before leaving, I approached the cabinet chief.

"As long as there is protection for Expedito, Carlos and Orlando, I don't need personal security," I told him. "I would not like to have armed agents of the Federal Police at my side. They would constrain me and might constrain people who needed to speak with me."

He nodded and made notes.

I went to the headquarters of the National Bishops' Conference, where

2. The OAB (*Ordem dos Advogados do Brasil*) is the national organization of attorneys. It has a reputation for advocacy of human rights—tr.

I was staying. Sister Alzira, as always, was fraternal and welcoming. João Batista, a consultant for the national office of the Pastoral Land Commission, was waiting for me. We had dinner with Memélia and with the Swiss journalists, Erling Soderstiom and Robert Blomback. During the meal they interviewed me.

We still had no news on the whereabouts of the peons. Today Dulce, a friend who works at the national headquarters of the Basic Education Movement, found them and took them to the attorney general's office.

Their audience with the attorney general, Doctor Aristides Junqueira Alvarenga, took place at 12:10. Hermógenes, known as Grandão, sat at the head of table in the attorney general's seat, but I spoke to him in time and he moved. I introduced myself and the two introduced themselves. Horácio was timid. Grandão didn't need any prompting.

"I was hired under false pretenses. They promised one thing and we got another. They deceived us with false hopes. As soon as we passed through the gate they began the beatings to break our wills. We were ordered to work without rest, even when sick. Two men got malaria and disappeared. They said that they sold the two of them to a ranch in Mato Grosso. But who would buy sick men? The poor guys were probably killed. One day I got sick. I couldn't work, and they wouldn't let me out for treatment. I cured myself with herbs and decided to get ready to escape. I had seen the foreman gather all the peons and force a sixty-five-year-old man to suck him, in front of everyone. I had seen a woman taken away from her husband and given to another. Neither she nor the man had any choice."

He then talked about his escape.

"I was preparing food. I was making plans to eat and get out of that hell. I saw a gunman coming. He ordered me to work. I said that I would not because I was sick. He threatened me. I picked up a big knife. He didn't want to fight me, so he went to get more men. I didn't have time to eat. I went deep into the woods. Then I crossed a stream, because water doesn't leave tracks. They came into the woods and fired shots above me. I was near them, within twenty or thirty yards, but they didn't see me. I was well settled in the middle of some leaves and water, with my ears open. One of the men said, 'He already got a beating, so he's going to talk. What if we catch him?' The other said, 'Kill him.' By night time I was far away from there. I traveled many leagues with an empty stomach. My clothes were getting torn, until I was practically naked. When night came I found some banana trees. I cut the leaves and made a bed. In the morning I found a road. I walked for a while, then noticed the footprints of two men. So I hid. I smelled danger. When I saw a farmer who was walking alone I asked him whether he had passed two men. He said that he had. Were they armed? He said yes. Once again I left the road. The hunger was tormenting me. I met a young girl and said, 'Daughter, is there food in your house?' She replied, 'Yes.' I had stuck my shirt into my belt, so as not to be indecent. My pants were in shreds. She said that her father was not home. I said,

'Child, I'm not asking for your father. What I'm asking for is food. Let's go.' She was afraid, but she gave me something to eat. I continued my flight until I got to Redenção."

Then Seu Horácio told his drama. He talked about seven months of work without receiving any pay, and about the violent scenes which he witnessed. Dr. Aristides listened attentively. Then I gave him the documentation that I had brought.

"Now that I have these documents," he said, "I will immediately order the Federal Police to open an inquest on the murder of the two young men on April 22. The assassins said that they were from the Federal Police. Do you think they were lying?"

"I suspect that they were not Federal Police," I replied.

"I will order inquests for the investigation of slave labor on the two ranches, with a priority on São Luís, since there are still workers being held there. These cases should be resolved by the state government, but there is an obvious omission. The picture is so serious that I consider federal intervention necessary."

The attorney general asked me to provide copies of the documents, including the pictures.

Some journalists were waiting for us in the press room, but time was short. We went straight to the airport so that I could catch my 7:30 flight. I asked Memélia to take the two workers to the Labor Ministry. We had tried in the morning to get an audience with the Minister of Agriculture and Agrarian Reform, Antônio Cabrera, but without success. So we filed a petition for expropriation of the São Luis and Arizona ranches. Then I was off to São Paulo to meet Heloisa for a meeting of the Faith and Politics Movement.

I talked on the telephone with Guaracy, who is following the development of the inquest in Rio Maria. He said that the police went to the Suaçuí Ranch, where they arrested the manager and three men who are suspected of working as gunmen for the ranch. They seized three rifles and a thirty-eight.

Friday, April 27. The meeting of the Faith and Politics Movement began tonight.

Heloisa and I got a ride to the Cajamar Center with Frei Betto, passing through São Bernardo.[3] He invited us to a debate that the factory workers had organized for the following night in the church hall in commemoration of Workers' Day. The speakers would be Vicentinho, president of the Union of Metal Workers of São Bernardo, and Paulo Vanucchi, a consultant for the union.

3. An industrial region of São Paulo, where in the early 1980s there was very strong strike activity—tr.

Saturday, April 28. About eight hundred people attended the meeting in the church hall. I heard that on some nights there were even more people. Vicentinho has a simple way of speaking, popular and direct, and he holds his audience. Paulo gave his contribution, and I also ended up being invited to speak about the land question and rural violence.

We are meeting in Cajamar until tomorrow night.

Frei Betto told me that Cajamar is an interesting place. It used to be a ranch. The owner built a kitschy chapel filled with plaster statues of various sizes, many of them related to Afro-Brazilian religious syncretism. In the sacristy we found dozens of statues that would not fit on the altar. After the ranch was sold, the place was turned into a motel, but the chapel was kept as it was. Later the motel was closed, and the area was changed into a center for meetings and courses for grassroots movements.

Tuesday, May 1. Yesterday morning I participated in the ethics seminar. In the afternoon I got together with some agronomy students from Piracicaba. Then I went to Santos to visit my brother Rogério and his family. Rogério came with me to São Bernardo for the Workers' Day mass, concelebrated by Dom Cláudio Hummes and several priests. The church was full and participation was intense. Many people carried banners and wore shirts with slogans defending the causes of factory workers, indigenous people and black people. There was a delegation from France, headed by a bishop. Lula and his wife Marisa were discreetly seated at the back. When the people learned of their presence, they became enthusiastic and sang Lula's campaign song, "Without Fear of Being Happy." Lula and Marisa were invited to come up front. Marisa was crying with emotion.

Dom Cláudio spoke about the struggles of the working class and made reference to the tenth anniversary of the surrounding of this church by the army, when helicopters flew over the place and important leaders of the union movement were arrested. The bishop invited Lula to say a few words. The whole congregation applauded and sang again. The French visitors were surprised that a former presidential candidate would speak during mass.

"He is no mere ex-candidate," Dom Cláudio explained. "He represents the greatest union leadership that this nation has ever produced. He did not speak as a candidate for any office; the elections are over. He spoke as a factory worker, a unionist and a Christian."

After mass, Frei Betto, Rogério and I went to the home of Marisa and Lula. I had first gotten to know them in 1980 in Morumbi, when the pope met with the factory workers. We saw each other on other occasions, and finally Lula went as a congressman to Conceição do Araguaia to participate in a demonstration for agrarian reform with a multi-party delegation of elected officials.

Marisa received us at the door of a spacious house, loaned to them during the campaign, where we could have a quiet meeting. We talked about their recent trip to Cuba and their impressions about the delicate political and economic situation through which that nation is passing.

Lula said that he does not intend to be a candidate for Congress in the next elections. He prefers to go to factories and to the streets, traveling throughout the nation.

"I don't have a vocation to Congress, talking to nobody, to empty and inattentive sessions, or having only Delfim and Roberto Campos for listeners. I want to dedicate myself to the Parallel Government."

14.

May 5 to May 13, 1990

In the aftermath of the April murders, the people who remain in Rio Maria are living in an atmosphere of constant threat.

Saturday, May 5. When I was getting off the bus in Rio Maria I met Dona Geraldina, Marciel, Carlos, Luzia and their little daughter Daniela. They were on their way to Belém, out of fear of being killed. They were sad, and so was I as I watched them leave. In this country the victims hide and the criminals walk freely, laughing at the tears of the survivors.

Isai invited me to have lunch with his family. Senhorina, the wife of his brother Washington, was there, talking about anonymous phone calls.

"They call the house asking for Washington by saying, 'Is the Dead Man there?'"

A wave of threatening phone calls has begun. In addition to Washington, Carlos, Expedito and I have been receiving them. Now that we finally have phones, they are being used as instruments of terror.

Roberto Neto attended the deposition of the three men from Suaçuí and recognized José Terezinho Vaz. He saw that man twice in Vila Nova, sometimes looking for Carlos, sometimes looking for someone else, armed and accompanied by another man.

Carlos's brother José Ricardo went with the police to Redenção. They wanted him to see the soldiers suspected of having participated in the murder of the Canuto brothers. José Ricardo thought that one of them looked very much like one of the gunmen.

Monday, May 7. João Bernardo of the Socialist Party is terrified. He, too, has received death threats by telephone. Antônio the teacher told me about a phone call that João Bernardo received in the early hours of this morning.

"They said that he was an agitator. They've already threatened Genivaldo (of the Socialist Party), my brother (City Councilor Sebastião Vieira) and Washington. People are afraid even to participate in a party meeting."

92

A few hours later I met João Bernardo in a bank.

"I've already received four threatening phone calls," he told me. "The first at one o'clock in the morning. I was sleeping and the telephone kept ringing. I didn't want to get up to answer it. Finally my daughter Glenia answered. She heard the voice of a woman saying, 'Shit! I want to talk with João Bernardo!' Glenia heard the voice of a man saying to the woman, 'We didn't get him this time.' Glenia heard more foul language before hanging up the phone. My wife answered the phone twice and heard that they were going to kill me."

I asked him if he suspected anyone.

"I have a certain suspicion. In one of the phone calls the man asked who is the PSB (Socialist Party) delegate for this city. I answered that I didn't know, but he knew that it was I. At that meeting that we had on April 23, after the burial of José and Paulo, there was a man who introduced himself as being from our party, but he was not. He was an agent for Police Chief Amaral. We discovered him and threw him out. But before leaving he heard me introduced as a delegate of the PSB. He must have passed on this information."

Dona Oneide, who is no longer the cleaner at the Cadete Pinheiro School, came to visit me. She has moved out to the countryside and is once again working the land. I found out only today that she is the sister of João Martins.

"There are a lot of people threatened, aren't there, Father? Carlos, Luzia, my brother, Isai and even you. It is sad to see people without convictions. They are afraid of the union, of everything. The power of fear is absurd. It even messes up elections."

She mentioned that former Police Chief Pedro Vieira has stated that he was dismissed because of me and that I am marked to die.

Thursday, May 10. João Bernardo has left town. Washington told me that the last phone call, on Tuesday, left João's whole family in panic.

"Who is this?" João had asked.

"You don't know me and you only have two days. You're going to die today or tomorrow. But don't worry. Maybe with your death the mayor will declare a holiday."

Recently Father Pedro went to Marabá. On the bus he saw the gunman Aprígio Meneses Soares. Since they've known each other for some time, he asked Aprígio where he was going. He said Belém. But two kilometers before Marabá, he got off with his baggage.

"Aren't you going to Belém?" asked Father Pedro.

"Yes, but I'm meeting some men who are going with me."

There is strong suspicion that Aprígio is involved with the April murders. I'm worried about Orlando. He is in Belém.

Orlando's brother-in-law Serafim, a short man with a straw hat, came to see me. He and his wife Aparecida live in Canaan, on Dona Geraldina's land.

"There were some suspicious meetings before the death of my father-in-law," Serafim told me. "One time I was coming into Vila Nova, when I saw several cars going to Valtinho's house. In them were Vantuil, Valter Valente, Adilson Laranjeira, Neném Simão and Doctor Alberto. This last one gave a party when they killed my father-in-law. I also saw Olívio, the owner of Canaan. One month before the assassination, I learned of another meeting, in Valter Valente's house. There were more meetings. The people on the street were commenting on that a lot during that time. They were saying that Neném Simão promised to give two million (US $202.94) and did not pay. Then Jurandir showed up in a new car. He was talking about having received, besides the car, ten million. The two men that he contracted received only three million cruzeiros."

Friday, May 11. Isai is jokingly calling his brother Washington JM for *Já Morreu* ("Already Dead") because of the phone calls. Washington has more information about João Bernardo. In one of the calls the unknown man asked, "What's the address of Sebastião, that agitator on the city council?"

"I don't know," João Bernardo replied.

"What's his telephone number?"

"I don't know that either."

"You do know it. He will die, just like you. You're not involved in land problems, but you agitate a lot around here."

"Here? Where?"

"In Rio Maria. I'm going to kill you."

"Why?"

"Never mind. You're going to die."

The murders and the threats have a political component. They are aimed at persons who could represent danger to the local powers. João Canuto, besides having been candidate for mayor, was president of the union. Brás was on the union directorate and a candidate for city council. Orlando is a present member of the directorate. João Bernardo and Expedito were candidates for mayor. Expedito is also president of the union, and Carlos is secretary. Roberto Neto is the local president of the PC do B. But there is still a question: Why did they kill José and Paulo Canuto? They were not farmers, they did not aspire to political or union office and they were not involved in grassroots movements. What was the logic that led to their murder? People around here talk about the meetings that planned the death of their father. They name names. Were the deaths a preventive measure? Did those who ordered the death of João Canuto fear vengeance from his sons? But why did they act only now? Why did they let five years pass? Perhaps because the sons were young at the time of the crime? Now the picture has changed. Amnesty International launched an operation demanding the conclusion of the police investigation, the functioning of justice. Dona Geraldina's family completely supported Amnesty's action. The Canuto case began to become a source of discomfort. Those accused of the crime walked past the sons of the dead unionist every day. There was an attempt to warn off the family last year with the irregular and arbitrary arrest of Orlando and Carlos. It was as though they were saying, "You may make noise, but we have the power. Leave the region while there is still time." Orlando gave the impression of understanding the message, because he moved to Goiânia for a while. But then he came back to see his mother.

Saturday, May 12. I was in Redenção, where I met a friend who said, "Ricardo, on the day of the burial of Brás and Ronan, I passed by a pizzeria, where I heard a strange conversation. As the funeral procession passed by a man said, 'More people are going to die.' Someone agreed with him and the owner of the place said, 'As long as there are invasions of property there will be more deaths.' Then a rancher said, 'All the communists must be eliminated. And that priest is a communist.'"

Before we said good-bye, he grabbed my arm and said:

"I have something to tell you. In 1986 I participated, by accident, in part of a meeting that dealt with the murder of João Canuto. I was in the house of a friend, where two liters of whiskey were being passed around. The principal topic was the death of Canuto. They decided that day to hire Jurandir. This was eight days before the murder. I went to see João and told him to run away. He refused to go."

"Were there many at that meeting?"

"There were twenty men, or more."

> Put your exhaustion to rest
> Seek lodging here
> Hang your hammock in this corner
> Rock your tiredness
> but don't forget your rifle
> arm yourself with courage
> prepare yourself
> The homely-faced ox[1] wears a hat
> he walks in groups and is well armed
> Who can save himself
> in the shelters of death?

> Ox
> Ox

1. The homely-faced ox (*boi de cara feia*) is a reference to a line in a lullaby — tr.

Ox of so much land[2]
overrunning the lands of farmers
invading their homes and stealing their hope
with fire

wake
wake
the big knife is entering your body

Sunday, May 13. A police officer came in and asked to talk with me alone. We went into the office. He introduced himself as Eleovaldo de Jesus Miranda de Souza and explained that he is a special officer, based in Belém, and that he was sent here to investigate recent events and the death of João Canuto.

"The investigation is totally irregular and is not accomplishing anything," he said. "We need to question the witnesses again."

I listened with curiosity. Was something finally going to be done?

"There are people connected with the crime," he continued, "with connections in Marabá, Itaituba, Abaetetuba and even as far away as Maranhão. Important people are involved in this, even government authorities. I worked in an office of people with prestige, in a very low position, in order to learn what was happening. Sometimes they even demand murder."

"There will be more deaths if the government doesn't act quickly," I said. "Those who have information know how risky it is to say anything, because of the complicity of the authorities with the crimes. So no one talks."

João Martins is not one of the silent ones. Today he came over, parked his bicycle, wiped the sweat off his face and told me the full story behind João Canuto's death.

"They say that there was a meeting to kill João Canuto. One with around twenty-five people at the house of Valter Valente. When the two gunmen arrived to shoot Canuto, they came from the Canaan Ranch, owned by Ovídio. Jesuino[3] rode into town on the same truck, but they didn't know who he was. So they talked freely about the police saying to Ovídio, 'If a *posseiro* comes to take land, you can kill him and bury him right where he falls.' The thugs were saying that they were from Goiás, that they knew Canuto and that his days were numbered. Jesuino went to the union to report what he had heard. Canuto was in Belém. When he came back, he filed a complaint at the police station. He hid in the house of Zé Alves and Dona Zulmira, while a city councilor went up and down the road by bicycle

2. The rhythm of these three lines imitates that of the lullaby: "*Boi, boi, boi, boi da cara preta.*" In this poem the ox is portrayed as an enemy because of the taking over of large tracts of land by cattle owners, who kill those farmers who resist them—tr.

3. Jesuino Pereira de Souza is an organizer of base communities and a former director of the union—tr.

about five times, trying to confirm whether Canuto was staying there and whether there were more people. Later he gave that information to the gunmen. After three days Canuto said, 'I'm not going to hide any longer. I'm going home.' Jurandir was there in the red light district, shooting pool. The gunmen were waiting. When Jurandir saw João Canuto, he left the pool table and spoke with him, in order to point him out to the gunmen. Seu João said good-bye to him and went to have lunch, unaware of what was about to happen. Later, when the shots were fired, Jurandir said, 'They killed Canuto.' He already knew. At seven o'clock at night, Jurandir picked the gunmen up in Campos Altos and drove them to Mayor Laranjeira's house. After midnight, he took them to Xinguara. They stayed in the house of Marcondes and Glória until the following day. During mass they were parked in front of the church in a white Chevrolet pickup truck, belonging to the Xinguara City Hall. They were waiting for Paulo Fonteles and Ademir Andrade.[4] Cláudia, my wife, had seen the two of them at Marcondes's house. She recognized them and said, 'Let's go tell Doctor Paulo and Congressman Ademir not to come out, because they could die.' I went and told them. They went out the back door of the church, passing through the parish house."

The telephone rang, interrupting the conversation. Afterward I went to get some coffee and put on a recording of Gregorian chant.

"Ademir said," João continued, " 'Set up a meeting with those women for tomorrow.' The women had information. The police had arrested Jurandir, who was their brother. The women arrived saying, 'We want to know whether you will get our brother out of jail, since he has nothing to do with the story.' The congressman was thrown off guard. 'Jurandir is your brother? I can't get that bandit out of jail. He left so many women widows!' The women got angry and left, saying, 'We should let them all die, because they won't free our brother.' Ademir had made a mistake. Instead of reacting as he did, he should have heard what they were going to say. On the day of the burial, the gunmen showed up in Marcondes's white VW. They were watching from inside the car, trying to spot Paulo and Ademir. They followed the funeral procession as far as the old cemetery, then gave up. Paulo and Ademir were in the middle of the crowd. If they had been on the edge they would have gotten shot.

"The murder of Paulo had been planned for a long time. One day, I think it was in 1984, I went to Conceição do Araguaia, where Marcondes had a house and a business. His wife, Glória, said to me, 'I'm so upset. They're going to kill Paulo Fonteles on Saturday during the inauguration of the Arraias Bridge. Call him.' I said to her, 'But I have to say who gave me this information. If not, he'll think it's only women's gossip.' She asked me not to mention her name, or she could be killed. I insisted that I could

4. Ademir Andrade is a former congressman and a member of the Socialist Party — tr.

not report such serious information without saying where it came from. So she told me that they were going to have a barbecue that night. Her husband would probably drink and end up saying everything. That was what happened. Marcondes said that he shouldn't be telling me this, but since I was part of the family, he would tell me: they had already hired people to kill Ademir, João Canuto and Paulo. Paulo was going to die the following Saturday. The price for the job had been set at five million cruzeiros."

A sound truck passed down the avenue, making conversation impossible. João sat back in the chair while I went to get a glass of water. The heat was unbearable.

"It was good money," said João. "Enough to buy some fifty cows. I asked him who was paying. He said he and five others."

"Did he give their names?" I asked.

"Yes. Besides him, the late Orlando Mendonça, his brother, who at that time was mayor of Conceição do Araguaia; Jordão, their uncle and owner of a business called Casa Azul; Elviro, who was elected president of the UDR in Xinguara; and Laranjeira, mayor of Rio Maria. He also said that Zanela, owner of the Riberão Novo Ranch, participated. He was the one who brought the gunmen from Paraná."

"Did you tell Paulo Fonteles?"

"The following day I went with Glória to the public defender in Conceição do Araguaia and we gave a deposition. The attorney communicated this to Paulo Fonteles, who was in Marabá, and to the judge. I gave another deposition before the district attorney, who was Orlando Mendonça's *compadre*. That document disappeared from the inquest. Then the judge was transferred and the new one didn't do anything. Anyway, Paulo didn't come for the inauguration of the bridge and so survived that time. Because of this whole mess Cláudia's family made it hard for us to stay together. So we separated, after eight years of marriage."

15.

May 15 to June 18, 1990

After all the tension in town, the travels through the rural communities seem relatively peaceful. Back in Rio Maria, the danger to Expedito intensifies. The owner of the Suaçuí Ranch is arrested in connection with the April murders.

Father Ricardo's preaching at the first communion mass and his guiding of a discussion during the parish assembly show the integration of his spirituality with his social mission.

Tuesday, May 15. Yesterday we celebrated mass in the Cristo Redentor community in Araguaxim, seventy-seven kilometers from Rio Maria. The chapel is in João Gregório's backyard. The house and the chapel have thatched roofs. There are a lot of fruit trees around the house, cooling the place. We slept at the home of Seu Hildebrando, next to a dense forest. The family seemed happy to put us up. They gathered wood, lit a fire, beat the rice and put the pots on the stove. I went to bathe with Hildebrando's two sons, carrying a lantern through a grove of mango, banana, guava and papaya trees. We passed between the wires of a fence and came to a clear stream. Free of dusty clothes, we went in, catching our breath because the water was freezing.

At the home of Antônio Branco we celebrated mass and the wedding of his daughter, Maria Aparecida, to Ismael Mesquita. They didn't rent a suit or a white dress, because they've already been living together and have a beautiful child.

Antônio takes pride in doing things well. He and his son-in-law made an enclosure out of poles and covered it with bleached white cloth from sacks of rice. They improvised some benches with green poles, gathered for the occasion. Little by little the people arrived, mostly on foot, some by bicycle. To my surprise I saw Helena, from the Cristo Redentor community, arriving with several people. After resigning from the coordination of that base community, she started two others. Every week she travels a considerable distance on foot, keeping the communities going. Today she brought the members of one of them to meet us. The mass was joyful, with Seu Hildebrando and one of his sons, Sérgio, playing guitars.

From there we went to São Sebastião II, where there was another wedding and the inauguration of a new chapel. The people had built it of wooden planks with a tiled roof and a cement floor. The walls were painted white and the windows brown. Little paper pennants crisscrossed beneath the roof. The whole community was happy with the construction. After the religious ceremony there was a feast, with plenty of food and dancing.

Wednesday, May 16. Early in the morning we drove to the Santo Antônio community. We stopped at the home of Édio, waiting for Chico Buchinho, who had sent a message that he would come for us. The road had been destroyed by the rains, and could be traveled only on foot or horseback. At 10:30 A.M. Chico arrived and tied the animals to the fence. Lunch was already on the table. After eating we set out. I was riding a mare that had a terrible way of bouncing. She was bruising me irreverently, and I was afraid of arriving at the end of the trip totally broken. Chico took pity on me and traded mounts. We crossed a lot of mud, ruts, dense forest, a pasture region and an area that was being cleared. They were planting the area and beginning to cut down the first trees. There was a lot of wood and leaves drying on the ground. Just a few more days and it would be ready to be burned. Branches and stumps made the crossing difficult. The horses walked slowly.

Early in the afternoon we sighted Chico's shack. Eva welcomed us joyfully, calling us to come inside. It is a tiny little house and new, with a roof thatched with tightly woven straw and covered with a large piece of plastic. The walls are made of sticks and decorated with calendars and pages from magazines strategically placed for privacy. The lady of the house called us to the kitchen. Another lunch! Could I refuse? They had killed a pig for us. We all served ourselves: rice, beans, fried chicken and barbecued pork. We filled our plates and returned to the front room. The house is divided into four parts: two bedrooms, kitchen and living room. I went to the earthen jug and dipped in a can to get some water. It was yellow.

Thursday, May 17. We drove to the community of Our Lady Aparecida. The road was a mess, even though it had not rained for several days. We had to do part of the trip on foot.

Saturday, May 19. There was a lot of hubbub at the home of Zé Almeida because of his daughter's wedding. They had slaughtered a cow, four pigs and eleven chickens. Some women from the surrounding area were helping in the kitchen. The men, besides killing the animals, prepared the place for the mass and the wedding. They improvised a table and benches, using some long boards. Friends of the bride made arches of bamboo and covered them with colored paper. The couple, filled with emotion, passed beneath these arches in the sight of many friends, relatives and curious people. When there is a wedding and an abundance of food and dancing, people come from leagues away. Today's host is one who never misses a feast. Wherever I go here in Araguaxim, when there is some feast, I always find Zé Almeida.

Tonight we celebrated mass in the Santa Catarina Chapel in Banápolis. The little wooden building was full. The people were anxiously awaiting the celebration of the Immaculate Heart of Mary. Twenty-four children, all in white tunics, formed a legion of restless little "angels" that came in procession from a house near the chapel. Each one carried a candle and sang heartily. The heaven of Banápolis had not only blond angels, but black, mulatto and indigenous ones. A heaven of diversity. At weddings it is common for the brides, regardless of their color, to come accompanied by little blond children. In Conceição do Araguaia, where there is a tradition of crowning the statue of Mary, the children used to be invariably blond. Dom Pedro Casaldáliga, on a visit there, commented on this during his homily. After that year the heaven of that city became more diversified. Here in the Santa Catarina Chapel a tiny black child, lost among the others, stood out at the time of the hymn singing because of her great voice. At the end of the ceremony we said good-bye to our friends and braved the road. It was 11:30 at night when I finally drove the car through the gate of the parish house.

Sunday, May 20. Today Sister Lourdes had a conversation with a lawyer from Marabá.

"I don't agree with you in everything," he said. "But what I will say is in your interest. In Ourilândia the name of Father Ricardo is known. People asked me to warn him that he needs to quiet down a little."

I went to visit Expedito, who arrived from Belém on Friday accompanied by a security officer. The officer, however, was not there.

"I could die at any moment," said Expedito. "I'm thinking of going to Belém and staying there for a few days. Things might calm down. As long as the gunmen and those who order them to kill continue to be free, we are at risk."

Expedito told me that on Wednesday the police exhumed the bodies of José and Paulo.

"Finally they're starting to act, after so many years of keeping their arms crossed. Crossed against us. Open for the landowners."

I was talking with Dona Francisca this morning, when a big man with dark hair and light skin, and with golden cords on his arms and chest, arrived. He introduced himself as Police Agent Augusto Silva and explained that he had come from Belém with Expedito to provide security for him. He wanted to know if I was threatened.

"They say that you talk a lot about land in church," he said.

"Less perhaps than I should. I may be too prudent, but I know that I'm dealing with dangerous people and I don't have reason to trust the police. I spoke with Minister Bernardo Cabral. He promised that certain people would have protection. And there is not a sign of it, after a month! Expedito got tired of waiting for security from the Federal Police, and he went to the secretary of public safety of Pará. With what result? They sent only one man for the task! While you're here talking with me, he could be getting killed."

"Yes. I was sent alone. I offered to sleep in his house, but it's small and there are a lot of people. Expedito himself recognizes that."

Tuesday, May 22. João Canuto's son-in-law Serafim came by again. He sat down timidly and held his hat between his hands.

"My mother-in-law is building a new house. Laranjeira offered materials. At first he offered the whole house. I was against it and so was Aparecida. A clay pot should not travel with an iron pan. Isn't that in the Bible? I prefer distance. But Carlos said, 'Let's take it. He owes her.' So Paulo went and accepted, but Laranjeira no longer wanted to give the whole house. He offered the materials and we had to provide the labor."

"I heard that you're planning to move."

"Yes, we're moving. Aparecida and I don't have land. Our plot is within *Comadre* Geraldina's and we are feeling in danger."

Wednesday, May 23. João Martins told me that the present police chief wants to move the investigation into the death of João Canuto ahead and has summoned him and Jesuino to give testimony. João is willing to do so but insists that it be in the presence of Sebastião Vieira and of me. I suggested that there also be a lawyer present. Today I telephoned Jorge Farías, lawyer for the PC do B in Belém, to ask him to help us find someone. He promised that someone would come on Saturday. He also said, "Someone left Belém early this morning."

Jorge did not explain who, and I did not ask, although I thought it might be Orlando. We both know that the telephone system has ears.

I stopped at the union headquarters and Expedito introduced me to others who were there. I sat on the rough bench and leaned against the wooden wall that was covered with posters defending agrarian reform and denouncing the deaths in the land struggle. I noticed that Expedito's hands were shaking.

"A lot of people are saying I should leave," he said. "I don't know whether I'll stay until Saturday. Even Officer Eleovaldo advised me to leave town."

"Protect yourself, my friend," I said. "Either leave or hide."

"I prefer to stay, because I have important information for the police inquest. I don't want to give testimony without the presence of a lawyer. Some of the testimonies have already disappeared, and I want to prevent that from happening. It was thanks to my testimony that they arrested the gunman Jurandir."

"How was that?" I wanted to know.

"Jurandir said, in front of a lot of people, that he knew the gunmen who killed Canuto, that he had been with them. I reported that. It was one more fact that led the judge to decide to arrest him."

Roberto came in with Sebastião Vieira, the city councilor. Sebastião had his little boy with him.

"I suspect that they hired Police Chief Pedro Vieira for the April murders," said Sebastião as he sat down and pulled his son into his lap. "When they arrested Orlando and Carlos last year he had the nerve to offer them money to incriminate Brás. Then last Sunday a colleague on the city council heard Pedro Vieira mentioning my name. I suspect that he's plotting against my life."

Sunday, May 27. The attorney from Belém didn't come through, but at the last moment the Pastoral Land Commission sent one of theirs, a young man named Joaquim. We were at the diocesan council meeting in Conceição when he arrived. Sister Lourdes went with him to Rio Maria. Joaquim was present when João Martins and Jesuino gave their testimonies in the parish hall.

I learned that Orlando was in Rio Maria on Thursday, accompanied by seven soldiers of the Military Police, to reconstruct what happened on April 22.

Monday, May 28. An armed man went into the hospital in Belém, looking for Orlando. Fortunately he had already been discharged.

Wednesday, May 30. Joaquim, the lawyer from the Pastoral Land Commission, gave me a copy of the police file on the death of João Canuto. It's a mess. There are some depositions, such as Laranjeira's, that appear twice, and others, such as the ones that João Martins and Jesuino gave shortly after the murder, missing.

Thursday, May 31. At the evening mass we remembered the tenth anniversary of the death of Raimundo Ferreira Lima, "Gringo." I remember coming back from Brasília, where I had reported that there was a list of people marked to die in São Geraldo, including Gringo, a candidate for president of the Union of Rural Workers. When I got back to Conceição, Heloisa told me that Gringo, who had just come back from São Paulo, had been wanting to talk with me. He waited for me until May 28, then left.

I headed over to the CPT office. Before going in I met someone who told me that Gringo had been killed in Araguaína before dawn.

A rooster tears open the night.
At three thirty in the morning.

The hammocks are gently swaying
with tired bodies.
Dona Maria do Pilar is already up.
She and her husband are making bread.
A rooster tears open the dawn
with his sad cry.
Itaipavas begins to awaken
beneath the attentive gaze of the river.
The memory of Gringo is alive,
alive is the voice that hesitantly described
dangers, stories of heroism and fear.
In this corner, facing the Araguaia,
he would tell me of the circle of the police, of flight.
"I was in hiding, prepared to die.
In the house the bishop and the priest were defending me."
The memories of the time of the guerrilla,
when the army created a nightmare.
Gringo, small, with thick-framed glasses and a gentle voice,
would laugh.
Today he rests a few yards away.
The aroma of coffee fills the house.
Voices fill the dawn.

Friday, June 1. João Martins was having a cup of coffee in the parish house.

"I talked with Chico from 13th Street. He told me that two of the gunmen who killed Brás arrived in town yesterday and are hiding at a ranch. Now listen to this: My wife, Eunice, left Belém on Tuesday at noon and got here on Wednesday. She told me that on the bus there were four men talking about the death of Brás, of the sons of Canuto and of Canuto himself. They were saying that 'more people need to die, especially the communists.' "

Saturday, June 2. Luzia called from Belém.

"Carlos went to the gold mines on the twenty-fourth," she said.

"I heard that a gunman went looking for Orlando in the hospital," I said.

"Yes. After that we changed our address."

Sunday, June 3. A man in a D20 pickup truck was near Expedito's house, asking for him.

Tuesday, June 5. I had just finished lunch when Father Hilário arrived. He was wearing shorts, rubber sandals and a cotton tee shirt. I pulled the cloth of his shirt to get a better look at the design: a black man breaking chains.

"How's it going?" I asked.

"Terrible. Awful news from the Jandaia ranch. On the twenty-fifth of last month a man escaped. He said that the owner had decided to cut down ten thousand acres, so he hired several gunmen and an enormous number of peons. Those who rebel, try to escape or ask about their salary, get killed, cooked and fed to the pigs. The report got to the City Hall and one of the councilors introduced the worker to Congressman Edmilson, who was passing through town. Edmilson took the man to Belém."

Wednesday, June 6. Expedito telephoned to tell me that there is an arrest order decreed for the owner of the Suaçuí Ranch.

"I was at the office of the secretary of public safety. I heard that the lawyers are trying to soften the order. They are promising that, if it is softened, he will appear."

He asked me to tell his family that he is sending some money.

Thursday, June 7. Expedito's son-in-law came to the parish house.

"My mother-in-law is not sleeping. She is so worried about all the threats hanging over Expedito that she wants to sell the land and go join him. If he telephones here, ask whether he'll give his authorization."

Friday, June 8. The newspapers from Belém reported the discovery of slave labor at the Jandaia Ranch in Xinguara. The manager had disappeared by the time the police got there. They found burned bodies and human bones in the pig sty.

This afternoon, while João Martins was visiting, Antônia, one of Expedito's daughters, came looking for me. Antônia is beautiful. She has the smile and the heart of her father.

"Do you know what happened just now while we were resting? I heard a car stop and the voice of a man asking if my father lives here. My little brother Fabiano said yes. The car drove away slowly. I got up and saw a white D10 pickup truck with an older white man inside. He was very big and sitting in the back seat. By his side was a black man. On the front seat there were two other dark men with straight hair. These three were young. I didn't think to check the license plate."

João Martins was listening attentively to what Antônia was saying. "I'll bet they were the same ones that my wife saw on the bus."

Tuesday, June 12. The telephone was ringing insistently. I was in the yard and ran inside to answer it. It was Expedito calling from Belém. I gave him the message from his son-in-law.

"He is asking for your authorization to sell the land, because Dona Maria is in agony. He said that the prospective buyer is offering 300,000 (US $3,448) and two cows."

"Tell Maria to wait a little. I'm not staying here long. We'll talk about it and decide together whether to sell the lot. I know she's afraid, but to sell the land means leaving here and doing what our enemies want."

He also said that he had news about the case, but couldn't talk about it over the phone. We said good-bye and he passed the phone to Orlando.

"Orlando, I'm so happy to hear you," I said. "How are you doing?"

"Fine. They're taking off the cast on the twenty-first. My arm hurts a lot, but that's supposed to be normal. My mother is also well."

"Expedito said that there was news."

"The case is going well," said Orlando.

Wednesday, June 13. Airton has taken time off from the seminary and returned to Rio Maria. He wants to take time to let his choice mature. He will be helping us with parish work.

Yesterday a group of people met to plan the first stage of the parish assembly. There will be two meetings. The first one will be here. It will include the base communities from Lower Rio Maria, of Mogno Road and of São Bento. The second one will be in Banápolis, with the Araguaxim communities. Father Hilário and Guaracy will serve as resource persons.

Thursday, June 14. Today is the Feast of Corpus Christi and first communion for some adolescents. During mass I thanked the catechists, who dedicated themselves during these months to the work of evangelization along the lines of the revised catechism, committed to life and history. I reminded the young people and the community that to receive the body and blood of Jesus is much more than a mere social event. It is to commit one's life, flesh, blood and history to the cause of the Kingdom. It is to put one's feet in the footsteps of the Lord, and these footsteps lead to the marginalized, the impoverished and the broken.

Jerônimo telephoned me from Belém.

"I was at the office of the secretary of public safety. It looks like they're verifying that there are at least four corpses at the Jandaia Ranch."

The telephone rang again. At the other end of the line was Patricia from Amnesty International. She asked me to go to Brasília on Tuesday. I accepted the invitation and dialed the regional seminary in Belém to tell Batista about the trip.

"Please find Expedito, Orlando and Jerônimo. Tell them that I'll be meeting with people from Amnesty International. If there is something important to tell them, ask them to let me know."

Friday, June 15. The peons who worked at the Arizona Ranch are worried. The foreman and the gunmen have been freed. They are saying that the foreman is threatening them. Father Aristide has notified the attorney general's office, and Guaracy has alerted the CPT lawyer Joaquim.

Since early this morning people from base communities have been arriving for the first stage of the parish assembly. There were people who came by public car, bus, bicycle or on foot. Each one contributed what he or she could: rice, cassava, flour, chickens. We all had lunch together. In the afternoon we formed two groups, one of farmers and one of people from town. I sat with the farmers. They talked about the paradox of a country with so much wealth and the people living so cut off from it. Dona Sebastiana offered an explanation.

"I think that the poor are poor because they don't economize. The president said on television that it is important to economize. The people don't obey. That's why there's such dreadful poverty."

I listened, then asked, "Are any of you rich?"

They laughed. They all said that they were poor, including Dona Sebastiana.

"According to what Dona Sebastiana said, you are poor because you don't save."

"What will the poor save?" said Dona Neném, from the Santa Luzia community. "My husband doesn't have money to take a bus from the countryside to the city. So he has to go on foot. Save? He wears out his shoes."

"Only the rich can save," complained Luís. "We eat rice and cassava without even the fat from meat."

"Poverty comes from the lack of administration in the country," said Jesuino, "and from the captivity in which the poor live. We live under great exploitation. Some of us work and don't have the means to live. Others don't work and have an abundance of riches."

"Our work isn't given value," added Dona Divina. "I brought thirteen cheeses to the market to sell. I got five hundred cruzeiros for them (US $5.76). That wasn't enough to buy even a package of sugar, which costs eight hundred."

Saturday, June 16. During the plenary session we asked the people to choose three priorities for parish work over the next two years. They decided on the training of community leaders, land issues and base communities. After Father Hilário explained the criteria for participation in the diocesan assembly, they elected delegates and alternates. We celebrated the closing mass with a lot of music and joy. The next stage of the assembly will be in Banápolis.

Sunday, June 17. The police have learned from the cowhand Mauro that Aprígio worked for the Jandaia Ranch, which was used as a general headquarters for gunmen. Mauro also reported that the Macaxeira Ranch supplied machine guns for this group and that, shortly after the death of Brás and Ronan, a box of tools appeared at Jandaia. Given the description of the box, Expedito suspects that it is the same one that the two mechanics were carrying on the night they were killed. The police invaded Jandaia, arresting four gunmen and a woman, but let Aprígio and the others escape.

Mauro revealed that the group of gunmen offered their services to other ranches. One proprietor from Curionópolis had hired them to do away with someone in Itaituba. When Orlando was called in by the police to identify the gunmen, he recognized one who worked for the Barreiro Preto Ranch.

Jorge Farias gave me additional copies of the files on the deaths of João Canuto and Paulo Fonteles and asked that I pass them on to Patricia.

Monday, June 18. Guaracy and I spent the whole morning preparing documents for Amnesty International. Then he drove me to the airport, where I caught the flight to Brasília.

When I got to Brasília, where I am staying at the apartment of friends, there was a message from Patricia saying that she was on her way. She soon arrived with the Senegalese lawyer Bacre Waly Ndiaye, vice-president of Amnesty International.

"We have an audience with the minister of justice," said Patricia. The appointment with Justice Minister Bernardo Cabral had been made from London.

We sat in the living room. Doctor Ndiaye does not speak Portuguese, so Patricia translated. I related the most recent facts, telling them that I suspect that the crimes have political motives and that they are connected to each other. The crimes are organized, possibly involving a number of ranchers.

Patricia telephoned the Ministry of Justice and learned that the minister would not receive us after all.

16.

June 20 to July 1, 1990

Suspicious occurrences around Expedito's house continue. Meanwhile, the gunmen responsible for the deaths of Brás, Ronan, José and Paulo are identified, and they further implicate Braguinha, the owner of the Suaçuí Ranch. There are additional visits from journalists and from representatives of Americas Watch. Father Hilário discovers more evidence of forced labor.

Wednesday, June 20. I was barely back home when Sister Lourdes told me that a strange man had gone to Expedito's house asking peculiar questions. We went there immediately.

The front room is small. From the street one can see straight through the kitchen to the backyard. The walls, which do not have plaster, are decorated by posters and pictures from magazines. There is a large dove, cut from cardboard, on which is written the word PEACE.

Expedito's daughter Antônia told us that at 2 P.M. on Monday a man appeared at the front door.

"He leaned in and said good afternoon. He was a dark-haired, light-skinned man over 40, with frizzy hair, a black hat, thick glasses, carrying a red bag and a black briefcase. I asked him to sit down. He asked for Father. Mother came in from the yard. She said that Father was away. Then he asked, 'How are the old ladies? Are they well?' Mother said no. Grammy was not well. She had a problem in her chest. He looked interested. He wanted to see Grandmother Maria and Aunt Isabel. He went over there saying nice words about justice. He presented himself as though he were a federal agent, a lawyer and a doctor who was going to prepare a remedy for Grammy. A very good one. Nothing better. He talked long and beautifully.

" 'Expedito doesn't have anything to do with the deaths,' he said. 'He is a different kind of man. We met in Brasília. We're bosom buddies. He likes to write poetry. And he told me about you, about the problem that you

109

have in your chest.' He opened the briefcase and showed the two of them a paper. They don't know how to read. He said that he had police clothes inside his bag. If they wanted to see, he would show them. 'We don't need to,' they said. And he wanted to talk with Father. At that point Negão, my brother-in-law, came in, and the man talked to him. After that he came back here. He called Mother and asked if she had a thousand cruzeiros (US $11.50). She replied that she did not. 'Couldn't you get a loan?' he asked. My mother said, 'Maybe from the priest.' He didn't like that idea. He wanted to know if there wasn't some other person, maybe a business-man. Mother said no. He said that Mother had to sign some kind of pro-vision for security for Father."

Dona Maria, Expedito's wife, brought in steaming coffee. The children came running into the room and she reprimanded them.

"He explained that in Brasília no one knows anything about these deaths," Antônia continued, "and that the federal government had come but had done hardly anything. But he was going to ask for six men from the Federal Police to stay for ninety days guarding Father. If Mother would sign the provision, Father could come back here safely. Mother explained, point by point, that she did not have any money and she did not know who could get any. So he said he would go to Belém to talk with Father. He asked for the address. Mother explained that Father was staying in the home of Neuton or of Neco. 'When will he be back?' he asked. Mother said at the end of next week. 'And the neighbors, they are not against him?' he asked. 'No,' Mother answered. 'They are all friendly people.' Aunt Isabel explained that when Father would arrive, he would go directly to the fields, because it's safer to stay outside of town. He wanted to telephone Father. 'What telephone do you use?' Negão said the one at the parish house. The stranger left, saying that he was in a hurry. Early in the evening we talked with Father. He thought it was strange."

I told them that they had been naive to have told him where to find Expedito, when he would return and where he was going.

"I saw the man at the bus station a while ago," said Antônia.

"Let's go there now," I suggested.

We stopped by the police station to get an officer to go with us to the bus station. We didn't find the man.

Expedito is worried about this story. I also talked with Orlando and with Luzia. They told me that Inspector Éder Mauro wants to know if Aprígio is in Rio Maria, because he needs to arrest him.

Thursday, June 21. Aninha called me from Conceição do Araguaia.

"I'm about to meet with two representatives from Human Rights Watch, Joanna Weschler and Jamera Ronee. Todd Crider, a student from Colum-bia University, will also be coming. They want to meet with victims of rural violence, with authorities and with us."

She passed the phone to Guaracy.

"The situation of the farmers is more complicated now," he said. "Out of forty-eight Land Reform Ministry employees in Conceição do Araguaia, forty-six have been laid off. We may as well be delivering all these cases of land problems to the cockroaches."

Saturday, June 23. On television the newscaster is reporting on the Amazon Forest: 8 percent of native plant life has been destroyed. With the death of Chico Mendes ecology has suddenly become big news. This is good, as long as the most important creatures, men and women, don't get left out.

Father Hilário came to Rio Maria to participate in a youth meeting. He told me that someone had learned from a deacon of the Assembly of God that there are children involved in slave labor near Marabá. Hilário was going to look for this deacon.

Sunday, June 24. Today Hilário pulled up in front of the parish house in an old jeep with the door held shut by a bolt.

"I talked with Deacon Adilson," he told me. "His church received a woman named Francisca, from Serra Pelada, who had been looking for her children, a girl of nine and a boy of ten. She sent them to buy sugar, and they never came back. She went to all the Assembly of God churches in neighboring towns, hoping that someone had news of them. She finally found them in the home of her married daughter in Redenção. They said that they had been kidnapped, taken to the Macaxeira Ranch in Ourilândia, guarded by dogs and gunmen and forced to work. One day they discovered that the dogs had become accustomed to them, so they ran away. They found a road, where there was a truck, headed south. The driver agreed to take them to Redenção. I asked the deacon, 'And what did the people of your church do?' He answered, 'The church does not get involved with these problems, except to pray.' "

Tuesday, June 26. Guaracy came from Conceição, bringing the representatives of Americas Watch and the student from Columbia. They talked with us, with the victims of land problems and with relatives of the victims. Early in the afternoon they went to see the judge, Doctor José Cândido de Moraes.

"Did you bring authorization from the Brazilian government for this type of interview?" the judge asked them. "If not, we may converse in generalities, but with no documents or tape recordings."

He began by saying that when he arrived in Rio Maria there were 332 cases pending, 35 percent of which were criminal. "Since then 567 new judicial actions have been opened. Out of these 21 percent are criminal."

The group had specific questions.

"Orlando and Carlos were arrested—"

"The district attorney asked for the arrest of those two," said the magistrate, "because they are accused of killing an employee of a ranch, whose name I do not remember. They were arrested illegally and so we freed them. They are suspects, however, and the inquest should proceed." He turned toward Guaracy. "Did you know Brás? He did not suffer any threat, neither he nor the Canuto brothers. There has been only one case of a request for protection. The directorate of the Union, after the deaths of April 22, asked for protection for the headquarters of the organization. They did not ask for protection for persons. I gave orders that a police officer should guard the building, as long as the workers considered it necessary."

"There was a lynching—"

"The lynching of Sebastião was a hideous crime, and the inquest concluded that the authorship of the crime was uncertain. About a thousand persons participated in the action and he was hit by about five hundred bullets."

"What about the April murders, Doctor?"

"It was all violent action and reaction against other violent action."

Guaracy could not contain himself. "Are you saying that the victims are suspects?"

"Yes," replied Doctor José Cândido, irritated. Then he went on to talk at great length about the absurdity of land invasions, the armed struggle in the region and the exchange of bullets.

"Did Brás, Ronan and the sons of Canuto die in an exchange of fire?" asked one of the members of Americas Watch.

"No."

"Are there a lot of gunmen in the city?"

"Yes. So many that it's impossible to count them. Several have been arrested. But in the invasions there is a lot of opportunistic banditry, invading just to get land to sell. An absurdity! There are people who need land, I recognize that. But there are people who only want money." He looked straight at Guaracy. "It is an ideological struggle."

Wednesday, June 27. Joanna Wechsler, Jamera Ronee and Guaracy left. Todd Crider stayed. We went to visit the Our Lady Aparecida base community, stopping to pick up three other people.

The sun was beating down on the road and the jeep was producing a terrible cloud of dust. We passed by some mining camps, went up and down little hills and passed through a herd of cattle. We arrived at an old headquarters of a ranch. We had taken the wrong road. We tried another wrong one. There was a stretch that the jeep could not pass through. We did the last four kilometers on foot, reaching the chapel late. The people were waiting for us, stretching their necks toward the road.

I introduced my companions. The people were especially curious about Todd, since he is North American. After hymn practice we talked. This community is passing through a difficult phase. Few people are attending liturgies, the readings are not being done well and the readers are being laughed at. No one from this community attended the parish assembly.

I was just getting out of the car in Rio Maria when the telephone rang. It was Isa Freade, correspondent from the Portuguese newspaper *Expresso*, calling me from Belém. He wants to come with a photographer to Rio Maria. I suggested that he first interview Orlando and Dona Geraldina, since they are in Belém.

Later I found a telephone message saying, "Isa the journalist says that the interview with Orlando was fantastic, and that the Canuto family is well."

Thursday, June 28. When I awoke this morning Dona Glória, Brás's widow, was already in the front room, waiting to speak with me. She is thinking of moving to Rio de Janeiro.

"I'm moving because my oldest boy doesn't want to live here any more," she said. "Since Brás died the garage has not had a single customer. I hired a mechanic, but it didn't work out."

"How old is your oldest son?" I asked.

"Seventeen."

She rubbed her hands. Dogs were barking in the street.

"I met Brás when he was a cowhand," she said with a catch in her voice.

"He worked at the Natal Ranch, didn't he, Dona Glória?"

"Yes. He began as a cowhand, then became a truck driver, transporting gas. He took a mechanics course and opened the garage. Brás liked to stay home with the children. He loved them all equally, but he gave more attention to the girls. He used to say that he took the most interest in them because one day they would get married and would suffer. But not the boys. They knew how to look after themselves."

"How are you surviving," I wanted to know, "now that there is no longer work in the garage?"

"I'm surviving with the little bit of money that I still have. I'm going to sell the house and the garage to buy a place in Rio de Janeiro and start my life over."

After lunch, Roberto Neto appeared. He arrived from Belém a short time ago. He was wearing closed shoes and a shirt tucked into his pants and was carrying a newspaper. A new mustache was trying to cover his lip.

"It looks like Brás and Ronan were captured by João Machado and Antônio Matador," said Roberto. "We have this information because, when the gunman Pássaro Preto was arrested, he talked. He accused Braguinha of having ordered the crime."

He also said that Aprígio was used for identifying persons who were to be killed and pointing out their houses. The main objective was to get the Canutos. On Tuesday the police took a sergeant and a soldier of the Military Police of the Marabá detachment to Belém. They were identified both by Pássaro Preto and by Orlando.

Airton, Sister Nehida and I went to Banápolis for the second stage of the parish assembly. The opening session began after supper. During the introductions we noted the presence of eight base communities and thirty-six participants.

Saturday, June 30. Today is the second day of the parish assembly. Some people prepared breakfast. Others swept the floor of the hall or went to get water. Sister Nehida, as quiet as ever, was hard at work helping the kitchen crowd.

The table was set with coffee, crackling, fried cassava meal and cookies. As we ate, cars passed by on the unpaved road, raising thick clouds of dust that invaded the school.

During the meeting we began by looking at the local realities. The communities have a lot to complain about. They do not have health centers, hospitals, physicians, medications, schools, teachers, roads or decent prices for their produce. We discussed this situation. Who dominates? Who is dominated? What are the consequences? How do the poor live? How do the rich live? What causes wealth? What causes poverty? What instruments are used to maintain this situation?

We referred to the book of James, which criticizes those who pile up riches and don't pay wages to their workers (5:4-5); it states that religion pure and stainless before God, our Father, consists in this: to take care of orphans and widows in their suffering and to keep oneself from being corrupted by the world (1:27). Which side am I on? My body can be on one side, but my heart, my will on the other. Am I split, incorporating within me the ideas of those who oppress me?

There are those who have power and who covet lands and houses (Micah 2:1-2); oppress the poor (Amos 4:1); sell the just for money and crush the heads of the poor in the dust of the earth (Amos 2:6-7); cast justice to the ground; are violators of the right of the poor in judgments (Amos 5:7b-12); therefore, hymns, celebrations, prayers that do not bring changes and conversion are not pleasing to God (Amos 5:21-24).

Sunday, July 1. We read the gospel text of Matthew 13:4-23, with the parable of the sower sowing the good seed, which falls on different terrains in the midst of rocks, by the side of the road, among thorns and finally on fertile soil. The reading was dramatized and some farmers represented the sower, the seed and the terrains. They commented on the parable and on the explanations of Jesus. They seemed impressed that the Lord affirmed that the thorns are "the cares of the world and the seduction of riches" that suffocate and kill the seed.

17.

July 4 to August 18, 1990

A poem by Carlos Drummond de Andrade sets off in Ricardo a reflection on love that ranges from the works of Saint Teresa of Avila to those of Brazilian novelist Clarice Lispector. The bishop comes for a visit, during which his attitude toward Ricardo and his work becomes evident. Later small farmers complain of harassment by IBAMA, the government agency that is supposed to be safeguarding the environment.

Wednesday, July 4. I got back to Rio Maria to find the journalists Isa Freade and Rogério Reis waiting for me. Tomorrow I'm going with them to Expedito's house.

Friday, July 6. I've been re-reading *The Body—New Poems* by Drummond[1] and came across this passage:

How imperfect our ways of
loving.

and does only love govern
everything beyond, everything outside of ourselves?

Absolute love
reveals the condition of flesh and soul.

That reminds me of the expressions of love and passion in the writings of the mystics. Teresa of Avila wrote about the gifts that God gave her in prayer, as a lover in the arms of the beloved:

1. Carlos Drummond de Andrade, *O Corpo—Novos Poemas* (Rio de Janeiro: Record, 1984).

115

. . . suddenly a feeling of the presence of God; in no way could I doubt that the Lord is within me, or that I am completely engulfed in Him.

Or:

First I had a continuous feeling of tenderness of which I believe that it is possible to obtain a part: a pleasure that is neither totally sensual nor totally spiritual: it is given completely by God.[2]

Clarice Lispector writes pages about the search for love, using language that is restless, devastating:

Surrender as I surrendered. Immerse yourself in the unknown as I immersed myself.[3]

I received a letter from my friend Trindade, who also sent me a copy of a letter from Father Henri des Roziers[4] and a copy of an interview that he gave in Guatemala to Father José Manuel Millan. They are two beautiful texts. He speaks of the tragic history of the indigenous and peasant martyrs; of the catechists, priests and sisters who have been assassinated; of the connection between mysticism and the struggle for justice. He talks about the fear, the church that does not always succeed in breaking through the wall of silence, and he reminds us of the extraordinary Bartolomé de las Casas, who lived intensely and unconditionally his prophetic compassion for the disparaged and the oppressed.

Thursday, July 12. Roberto Neto told me about a conversation with Inspector Éder Mauro.

"He told me that the police officer Ubirajara confessed to having participated in the murders on April 3 and 22. Sergeant Matos acknowledged his participation on the twenty-second. He also learned that the Santa Helena Ranch has a blue VW beetle and a D10 pickup truck. The pickup was used during part of the kidnapping. The gray Gol that was used belongs to former police officer César, who lives in Curionópolis."

A gentle light was filling the late afternoon when Expedito came to the parish house. He extended his hand. In spite of so much oppression, he still maintains his smile.

"I suspect," he said, "that Pássaro Preto has worked for Neném Simão

2. *Autobiography of Saint Teresa*, trans. Rachel de Queiroz (São Paulo: Loyola, 1984). Portuguese edition.

3. Clarice Lispector, *A Lesson or The Book of Pleasures*, 17th ed. (Rio de Janeiro: Francisco Alves, 1990).

4. A French Dominican who has a law degree and worked for the Pastoral Land Commission of the Araguaia-Tocantins region from 1978 through 1990 — tr.

and several other ranchers. I discovered that Antônio Matador was looking for Brás in his garage and also came to the union headquarters."

Wednesday, July 18. I had barely finished breakfast when Luzia came in, her eyes red from lack of sleep. She and Carlos had just come by bus from Belém and were traveling with us to the house of Leandro, Carlos's father.

We passed by the Santa Luzia community and turned onto a side road. We crossed a wooden bridge over the Maria River. For the rest of the way we followed an irregular and difficult path.

We reached the home of Carlos's parents, left the couple there, and continued to the Our Lady Aparecida community. The passage was through the woods, with a lot of undergrowth. I was able to negotiate the last few kilometers only by acrobatics with the steering wheel. Erasmo was waiting for us, but was not expecting us for lunch. At 1 P.M. the meeting began. My empty stomach was protesting.

We returned to Seu Leandro's house, where we had a very late lunch, then celebrated mass. They prepared a table beneath the trees. Seu Leandro's daughters, who are nuns, arrived from Tocantins and from Mato Grosso.

I slept well that night, after a hard day, and awoke to the call of the roosters. We returned to Rio Maria today.

José Batista has arrived for another pastoral internship.

Saturday, July 21. I visited Expedito at the union office. Since there weren't many people there, we were able to talk. He expressed again his worry about the risks that he was running.

"Ricardo," he said. "The one who was at Brás's house before April 3, according to the description of Mauro the cowhand, was Antônio Matador. After being expelled from the Military Police, he continues to turn the lives of the poor into hell."

Sunday, July 22. There was a meeting of the Brazilian Popular Front in the Rocha Theater at 10 A.M. Various candidates were in the city. After lunch, several members of the Front, including Almir Gabriel and Ademir Andrade, stopped in at the parish house. The living room seemed smaller than ever with so many people. Senator Ademir was talking about the campaign's economic difficulties. I had not seen him for some time. Later he came over and talked to me.

"Ricardo, I was really annoyed that you didn't accept the nomination for deputy governor on our slate."

"Well," I said, "that would have required strong interest and a certain knack—"

"You've got a knack!" cut in Almir Gabriel.

Everyone laughed.

Tonight we will have a solemn mass for the confirmation of several young people. The bishop arrived this afternoon, wearing a huge hat with a string that fell from both sides and came to a bow beneath his chin. He was walking with a cane, having not yet completely recovered from a recent fracture. He also looked thinner. Dom José uncovered his white hair and said that I did not need to worry about lunch, since he had eaten in Redenção. I took him to his room so that he could rest a little.

Tonight twenty-one young people were confirmed in a beautiful ceremony. I was thinking how unfortunate it was that they placed so much importance on special, expensive clothing.

Monday, July 23. In the morning I went with Dom José to Santa Luzia. Sister Lourdes and João Batista had gone ahead to get the people from the various communities of Lower Rio Maria to come to be with the bishop and to participate in the mass. We parked the car in the shade and went into the new wooden chapel. People had cut papers to make little pennants. The decorations were crisscrossed under the roof. Dom José put on white vestments, leaned against the table and conversed with the people. He talked to them about Jesus and put out a question.

"Why did Jesus come to earth?"

There were a few seconds of uncertainty, timidity. But little by little some voices spoke up.

"To save."

"To teach."

"So that everyone would have life in abundance," said the teacher.

"That's it," said the bishop. "I was waiting for that answer. Jesus came so that all would have life in abundance. So he healed the sick and showed mercy and compassion. In relation to the Pharisees he was hard."

He gave a sermon linked to the reality through which the nation and the region were living. He gave evidence of the existence of illnesses, some deriving from water contamination. People must organize to confront this situation. Making demands by oneself, in isolation, does not get one far. He reminded us of the electoral process and of the need for a conscious and free vote.

A young girl who was not from this community got up and left, saying in a loud voice that the church should not talk politics.

Tonight we had a meeting with fifty-two young people. Dom José told them that they could ask any questions that they wanted. They asked him to talk about the relationship of the church to politics.

"Politics is promoting the common good," said the bishop. "Those who condemn the church for speaking about politics are those who have privileges and are afraid of losing them. Or they are poor people with the mentality of the rich. To speak about transforming the society creates discomfort and requires commitment. To participate in the Eucharist is also to participate in transformation, in the desire for a better life."

Wednesday, July 25. Yesterday Dom José and I celebrated mass in Banápolis and early today had a meeting with forty-eight representatives of the Araguaxim communities. The meeting took place beneath some trees in the backyard of Roberto's house in São Sebastião II.

Zim, from the Triunfo community, raised a concern about the accusation that the church is getting involved in politics because it defends the farmers. Dom José reminded the people that property is a right, not a privilege for a few. He quoted Pope John Paul II, who stated, "All private property carries a social mortgage."

Thursday, July 26. Back in Rio Maria, Dom José met with the land team. He began with questions. Why this team? Does the church have something to do with land?

"If we're disorganized, we're going to lose the land," said Jesuino. "The Land Team can help."

"Some think," said Luís, "that land and church have nothing to do with each other. They are wrong. God wants a more just world, and the church cannot hide its eyes from our troubles."

"The Land Team should not enter into a conflict as though it were the police," said Edmilson, "nor place the farmer, as though it were the Land Reform Ministry. It serves to support people in their doubts."

"The larger forces swallow up the smaller ones," said Jesuíno. "The poor by themselves don't have the means to eliminate poverty. The church cannot stay outside. Aren't we the church? And we depend on land!"

Dom José had been listening in silence. Now he spoke up.

"You said it well. We are the church. And we depend on the land. To want to stay on the land, working in peace and prosperity, is a legitimate and necessary desire. The institutional church by itself is not interested in land. It is interested in persons. It needs to preach the good news of Jesus Christ to you; it wants to be in solidarity with your sorrows; it wants to serve. It knows that for you to live better, you need land, schools, health care. If you remain passive in the face of the gunmen who come to throw you off the land, you will die. There are few organizations as poorly understood as the Pastoral Land Commission. Ricardo has experience in this type of work. You are in the hands of God and in his hands. Those who want him dead are the same ones who want the 'liberty' to oppress others."

There was a moment of silence. Then Jesuino spoke up.

"Those who assume this responsibility know about the risks. But, as Christ said, 'Whoever wants a quiet life will lose it.' Those who are prepared to lose their life for Him and for the gospel, will save it."

"This is an important moment for you," said the bishop.

Friday, July 27. Tonight the bishop had a meeting in the parish hall with forty-eight persons representing the various parish teams. They introduced themselves and explained the type of activity which they are developing. Some members of the charismatic prayer group were also there.

"How does the church see us?" they asked the bishop.

"You may continue to meet," he replied, "but you should be aware of four dangers: becoming an isolated group of 'saints'; exaggerating miraculous cures; not accepting the need for social transformations; becoming isolated from the context of social-pastoral work."

Wednesday, August 1. A group of us gathered in Conceição today to hear reports of parish assemblies and to make the final preparations for the diocesan assembly which begins tomorrow.

I got together with Father Hilário. He told me about his recent trip into the countryside.

"I went to celebrate mass with the base community of Pedra Bonita. Afterward, while I was taking off my vestments, I heard an argument. Ângela, daughter of Sinhá, who is the leader of the community, was furious with Maria da Luz. I learned that, last year, the night of Ângela's marriage to Pretinho, there was something going on between Maria da Luz and her husband. Apparently the two were rubbing against each other. Da Luz, a pretty young girl, fair and with a graceful body, was denying it. Ângela, who is dark and also attractive, did not believe her. The rest of the people were split. Things were really heating up. Finally one man suggested, "Why don't we just ask Pretinho?" It happens that Pretinho is a dangerous gunman, which neither Ângela nor Dona Sinhá had imagined at the time of the wedding. They thought that he worked at clearing land on ranches. Actually he was hired for killing. He's quite a sleazy guy. He appears simple, with his felt hat, high boots, gentle speech and humble origins. Well Pretinho turned into quite the wildcat. He pulled out a big thirty-eight and pointed it toward the people, getting satisfaction out of threatening them. Everyone was screaming. One woman passed out. I was thinking, 'This nut is going to kill someone!' So I jumped on him, struggled with him and got the weapon out of his hand."

I looked at Hilário. He's lightly built. He looks like a little boy.

"Weren't you afraid?" I asked.

"Did I have time to be? I thought of what he might do and acted. Afterward, yes, with the weapon in my hand, with the situation under control, I did start shaking."

"How did Pretinho react?"

"He was furious, but what could he do?"

Thursday, August 9. Early in the morning Expedito came by with two farmers from São Roque—Carlos Roberto, a man of less than 30 years, and Claudiomar, a married man, father of six, who has been working on 120 acres for six years.

"It's getting tense these days," said Expedito, "with IBAMA harassing the people."

I invited them to come in. We sat in the kitchen and passed around a thermos of coffee.

"The harassment began Saturday," said Claudiomar. "Tell it, Carlos."

"Around 2:30 in the afternoon a D20 pickup truck stopped beside me. I saw five men: one short guy with white hair, three with vests and thirty-eights, and one with what looked like a machine gun. I saw a guy who resembled Neném Simão's family. I was even more scared when another car pulled up. It was an F1000, dark purple, almost black. I think it belongs to the same Neném Simão. I was scared and suspicious when I noticed two men in the cab and three soldiers of the Military Police in the back of the truck, armed with rifles. They took my chain saw, and they ordered me to sign a paper to appear tomorrow in Xinguara, at IBAMA. I was angry. They invade houses, even when people are not home. In Chico's house they took a snakeskin. They went into Zé Milonge's shack and took a deerskin and a lantern. At Joel's they carried off a scythe, a spade, a pickaxe, a knife, a hoe and shears. I know that they went into fifteen houses. They used my son and another boy as guides."

"They brought Irineu here to Rio Maria," said Expedito. "And Neném Simão's son accused him of stealing fencing wire and killing a peon. The police chief hit the farmer twice in the face. He ordered Irineu to find me and bring me to the police station."

"Mayor Tião Aranha said that he talked with the people from IBAMA about the clearing of land," said Claudiomar. "They said that the farmers could clear up to thirty acres without permission."

Expedito was doubtful. "I think he was misinformed. The law gives authorization to those who have title to the land. Does the poor farmer have title? The farmer does the work. He improves the land. The law is unjust. Whoever can pay can clear the land."

"The mayor promised to participate in a meeting tomorrow," said Claudiomar.

"Are you going to that meeting?" I asked.

"Not if I'm going to be ordered around," replied Claudiomar. "I'm not crazy. Imagine—IBAMA said that Neném Simão will participate! We'll be obliged to negotiate and leave the land. We have been there, working it. But he has the papers."

"It's absurd," I said. "IBAMA is supposed to be there to take care of ecology, not to favor the land claims of speculators. And what is the point of taking someone's tools?"

"Where does Neném Simão get the moral authority to come in with IBAMA," said Expedito with irritation, "fining the farmer for clearing land? He is a lumberman, the worst enemy of the forests. He takes thousands of cubic yards of lumber from the lands of the Gorotiré Indians, right under the noses of the authorities. They are using IBAMA to throw out the farmers so that they can get the land. We have proof that he already tried to cut down a lot of trees in this area. The union telephoned the Land

Reform Ministry, informing them of that. I mailed a report to the union federation and to Congressman Ademir Andrade."

"Wouldn't it be good to get a lawyer for this?" I suggested.

"Yes. I talked with Jorge Farias. He promised to send a lawyer."

Saturday, August 11. Orlando arrived in Rio Maria without any protection, despite the fact that there must be a lot of people interested in seeing him dead, since he is a key witness in the investigation of the murder of his brothers.

Monday, August 13. We left after lunch for São Geraldo. The roads are tortuous. There are ninety kilometers without pavement.

We passed by a desolate landscape with hundreds of dead Brazil nut trees. When alive these trees are huge and beautiful. Now they are dry, with black limbs charred by fire, branches without leaves, reaching to the sky like the nervous arms and fingers of sculptures that symbolize destruction. The law protects these trees. They cannot be cut down. The ranchers obey partially. They don't cut down these trees, but they cut down all the trees around them and set fires which invariably destroy them.

We finally arrived in São Geraldo. There was a guerrilla movement here from 1972 to 1974, and the civilian population, without understanding what was happening, was permanently marked by the police repression which came down on the region. Fear and accusation became part of people's daily lives.

The gathering began with sixty base community leaders. Sister Lourdes and I came to serve as resource persons. The proposed theme was very broad: capitalism, socialism, communism, terrorism. The people are intimidated by these words that the Army and the ranchers frequently use, and they want to know what they mean.

"O.K.," we said to the participants, "they use them a lot. But do they explain them?"

"They say that the church is communist, terrorist. They say that that means to kill, steal, take the wife of another and make terror."

"And has the church done any terrorizing here? Has it killed? Robbed? Taken somebody's wife?"

"No, they're the ones who do that."

Thursday, August 16. A thin layer of ash fills the city, covering and invading the houses, piling up on the beds, in closets, on the floor. The sun turns into a red ball, and the blue of the sky disappears behind the smoke. Eyes become irritated. The flames devour the forests, invade the pastures, kill animals and plants and pollute the waterways, killing the fish. The burning continues unabated, despite lectures from the government. This large-scale destruction goes unpunished by IBAMA, which is understaffed and is still wasting time fining the small farmers.

Saturday, August 18. Maurice Lemoine, a French journalist, arrived today. He plans to write an article for *Le Monde Diplomatique* and a book about the land problems. I told him about forced labor on the large ranches, land conflicts and the neglect by the government. I took him to the union office, where he interviewed and photographed Expedito.

18.

October 20, 1990, to February 9, 1991

The period from September 1990, through January 1991, appears to have been relatively uneventful. Among the few noteworthy things that occurred during that time were Orlando's visit to Paris, the auditing of the books of former Mayor Laranjeira, and the growing sense of threat surrounding Carlos Cabral. At the beginning of February, however, there occurred one more act of violence that would call the attention of the world and would leave a permanent mark on Rio Maria.

Saturday, October 20. Orlando went to France to testify at the Permanent People's Tribunal, denouncing the violence of the landowners. On his return he telephoned me from Rio de Janeiro.

"I enjoyed the trip," he said. "It was good in terms of denunciations. I brought a lot of material for the jury. But I wasn't happy about the verdict. They did not find the Brazilian government guilty of genocide."

"Who was there from Brazil?" I wanted to know.

"Alfredo Vagner, who worked in MIRAD, Father Ângelo Pança, from Barcarena, Davi Yanomami,[1] Osmarino[2] from Acre. They all brought documents. There were thirty minutes for the denunciations. After that I talked with people from television stations from various countries, and also met with someone from Amnesty International. I met people who are important for our struggle, including some from Labor Confederations."

"It sounds like you enjoyed it and that it was worthwhile."

"But one thing didn't agree with me. In these five days in Paris I lost six pounds. Their food is very strange."

Sunday, October 21. I was listening to the song, "Paul Gauguin adored the light in the Bay of Guanabara" when Carlos came in looking

---

1. Representative of the Yanomami Indians of the Amazon — tr.
2. Successor to Chico Mendes as president of the Union of Rural Workers in Xapuri — tr.

worried. He said that he was followed yesterday while passing through the red light district on his way home to Vila Nova.

Wednesday, October 24. The city council is buzzing with the audit of the accounts of former Mayor Laranjeira. When he took office, he had thirty-five head of cattle. He left office with hundreds. The nine councilors have turned against Laranjeira and are doing a judicial inquiry.

Friday, November 9. Carlos is letting his beard grow. Sometimes he changes his appearance, thinking it will confuse the gunmen. I don't know if it works.

"My family is worried," he said. "But I won't rest until I discover everything about the murders. I'm going to stay in Rio Maria to investigate all this. The authorities aren't interested. We workers are."

Saturday, November 10. Airton came from the post office with two large envelopes. One sent by Rogério Reis from Rio de Janeiro contains the article published in the Portuguese magazine *Expresso*. It's a long piece written by Isa Freade with photographs by Reis. I opened the other envelope. It was the Swedish *Kommunal*, with an article written by the reporters who attended our meeting with Justice Minister Bernardo Cabral, shortly after the death of the Canuto brothers. The article in *Expresso* is well written. I don't understand the Swedish publication, but the pictures are beautiful.

Tuesday, December 18. Today is the fifth anniversary of the death of João Canuto.

I received two issues of *Le Monde Diplomatique*, for October and December. In the first there is an article entitled, "Christ Recrucified—Priests Assassinated in Latin America," with the subtitle, "The Silence of Pope John Paul II." In the other issue I found "Land Conflicts in Amazonia— The Brazil of the Men Marked to Die." They included three pictures, one of Expedito, one of Pedro from the Carlos Drummond community and the last of the gunman Neto and his brother, showing their weapons. The articles are long and were written by Maurice Lemoine.

Friday, December 21. The gunman Geraldo, who killed Father Josimo, has escaped once again. After his previous escape, he hid in Tocantins, where he attacked a woman, which resulted in his being arrested again and taken to Gurupi. On November 14 the police chief there informed the prosecutor that the jail was not secure. The prosecutor requested a transfer, but the judge denied it and scheduled a hearing for November 30. Many organizations sent telegrams to the governor of Tocantins and to the secretary of public safety, asking for the transfer. The governor himself sent a telex to the judge, insisting on it. Congressman Luís Eduardo Greenhalgh spoke in a congressional session, saying that, if there were not a transfer, the gunman would escape. On November 28 he did.

Tuesday, December 25. Last night at ten o'clock we had the Christmas mass. This is the time to reaffirm hopes, the time of urgent persistence, the time of the Word that was made Flesh!

> Be born, Child, be born,
> be born on this clear night
> in the silence of this hour.
>   AND
> blessed be the joy
> of the fruit of the womb that is announced!
>   Today and always!

Saturday, December 29. I arrived in Juiz de Fora at lunch time and found the family all together. My father and mother looked happy in the presence of their children, daughters-in-law, son-in-law and thirteen grandchildren.

Tuesday, January 29. I've been taking full advantage of the holidays. Eleven months of furious work and one month for more playful activities. I went to Rio de Janeiro, spent time with good friends and took in several films, art exhibits, a play and a concert. Later we celebrated the Feast of the Kings.

Thursday, January 31. Father Henri des Roziers visited me at my parents' home in Juiz de Fora. After all his years of dedicated work as a Dominican priest and as an attorney in our regional office of the Pastoral Land Commission, he is on his way to Guatemala. We're going to miss him a lot.

Friday, February 1. I'm traveling to Belo Horizonte, where I'm going to meet Heloisa, since we're taking the same bus back north.

Monday, February 4. In Belo Horizonte I also met Angélica, who was coming with us to get to know the work of the Basic Education Movement in our diocese. She is thinking of working in Conceição do Araguaia.

We crossed the states of Minas Gerais and Tocantins, and at 5:30 on Sunday morning passed through the town of Peixelândia. All we had to do then was cross the bridge over the Araguaia river and we would be in Conceição. Suddenly the bus stopped. I saw our friend Miriam getting on.

"What are you doing here?" I asked, startled out of the drowsiness of a short night's sleep.

"Get your bags and come with me," she said.

"But I'm going to Rio Maria. I'm not stopping in Conceição."

"You can decide about that later. Get your bags and get off."

Miriam woke Heloisa and Angélica. We got off the bus. The Toyota jeep was parked by the side of the road. Heloisa, unable to contain her nervousness, asked Miriam what was going on. We got into the jeep and Miriam said:

"They killed Expedito last night."

The shock was tremendous. I felt as though I had been shot along with him. I immediately thought of the murders of Josimo, Paulo Fonteles, João Canuto—the cycle of "announced deaths," as the international press had printed in boldface. In December *Le Monde Diplomatique* had published Expedito's picture and had cried out about the death threats. Other national and international newspapers and magazines had put out the same alarm. In vain was our meeting with the minister of justice. In vain was Expedito's meeting with the secretary of public safety. Had Rio Maria gone mad? Had the nation gone mad? The local judge, indifferent to what was happening, had declared, "The index of violence in this town is far less than that of the periphery of Rio de Janeiro." But our situation was different from that of urban violence. We were up against political assassinations. Whoever dared to dream about a better world was getting killed.

How was Dona Maria José, Expedito's wife, taking this? What about the nine children? What about his mother and his sister?

Was this going to be another uninvestigated crime? Would there be another inquest that would gather dust on the shelf in the police station? Would the whole city once again speak the names of the assassin and of those who paid him, everyone knowing the facts of the case? Would the federal, state and municipal authorities once again remain indifferent? Would they feign a mournful air, without outlining any measures to put the brakes on the violence? Or would they blame the victim for his own death?

Expedito, how fitting is your poetry, written for a fellow Brazilian:

On that ill-starred day/Nature groaned
All joy disappeared/Brazil was convulsed
The world was jolted/The waters swirled.
The Amazon mourned/The earth was cloaked in grief
When the news was heard/Of the death of Chico Mendes.

"Expedito was shot three times about two hundred yards from his house," said Miriam as she started the car. We've been here since 1 A.M. We came to wait for you because of a phone call that we got from Rio Maria, from Sister Lourdes. Ricardo, a soldier told her that someone was planning to kill you this morning before you got into town."

We went directly to the Pastoral Land Commission office, where people had spent the night in vigil, keeping in touch with Rio Maria and answering calls from everywhere.

I went to see the bishop, and we arranged for his presence at the funeral mass. Then we traveled in two cars to Rio Maria.

When we reached the church I saw a crowd of people in front. Expedito's body was being waked under the thatched festival canopy beside the church.

"This is where the people wanted it," Sister Lourdes told me. "It's cooler than in the church."

I got out of the car and went into the festival area. It was full of Expedito's friends — rural workers, housewives, students, gold prospectors, some small businessmen, teachers, public servants. All were silent. I went near the coffin but didn't want to look at Expedito's face. I wanted to remember him smiling, riding his bicycle in the streets of the town and on country roads. I wanted to remember his serene, low voice and his characteristic gestures. I wanted to remember him sitting in the union office, attending to the needs of the farmers and reciting his poetry.

Later we went into the parish house. It, too, was full of people. The telephone was constantly ringing. I had a sense that this one assassination would have greater repercussions than the dozens of previous deaths. After Chico Mendes, national public opinion had become more sensitive and the media were paying more attention.

I went to Expedito's house and found Dona Maria José in the kitchen, crying. Her mother-in-law, her hair covered by a white kerchief, was leaning on her cane, moving her feet with difficulty. There was a certain calmness about her. She had lost other children and her husband. Had she learned how to get through times like this? Or was she being sustained by her faith and her special devotion to Our Lady Aparecida, the Black Madonna, a saint of her own color? Expedito's sister Isabel was silent, holding in her deep sorrow. At such moments words become especially difficult. We're not dealing with cold, distant statistics, but with dear friends who have been wrenched out of their everyday existence.

Expedito was one of the few people who really lived the biblical mandate:

"If someone wishes to come after me, he must deny his very self, take up his cross and follow in my steps. Whoever would preserve his life will lose it, but whoever loses his life for my sake and the gospel's will preserve it" (Mark 8:34-35).

Later during the funeral mass I was looking at Expedito's family, seated in the front pew: the grown daughters, the younger children, his son-in-law, Dona Maria José in a plaid skirt, sleeveless white blouse and rubber thong sandals, her face covered with sorrow, a drenched handkerchief in her hand. On the floor the youngest child was sleeping, and the grandson, his eyes as big, round and dark as jabuticaba fruit, was watching the movements of a photographer. In the second row I could see the agony in the face of Dona Isabel, whose head was wrapped in a white kerchief that completely covered her graying hair.

I was thinking at that moment how, for Expedito, salvation wasn't an individual project, narcissistically constructed for himself. It was about opening up to others and delivering oneself to the risks of the Kingdom of God. Expedito wanted to live intensely. He also wanted to ensure that everyone else would live. He held dreams that the big landowners despised: democracy, healthy children, farmers getting the earth to produce basic necessities. He delighted in those bright hopes, and that caused discomfort for those who did not want to be distracted from the horizon of their own wealth.

During mass the elected officials arrived from Belém, along with the forensic specialist. He took the body from the church for examination, while the ritual continued. Afterward Roberto, Carlos and other political leaders organized a protest demonstration in front of the church.

Because of the threats and the lack of light at the cemetery, I thought it prudent not to go. As I was closing up the church I met Carlos. He was tense. He had spoken with a man named Chico, a cowhand who was on Expedito's street at the moment of the crime and saw who killed him.

"I asked him to describe the assassin," said Carlos. "Then I went looking for him. I saw someone who looked like him right here in front of the church. I went to get Chico to make sure that he was the one. I reported him to the police chief, who showed a complete lack of interest. He's going to let him get away!"

When the politicians came back from the burial we asked them to go talk to the police chief. I later talked with Chico, the cowhand who had witnessed the murder.

"It was night," he said, "and I was talking with a friend on the corner of Tenth Avenue and Seventeenth Street. Expedito passed by. When he had walked about another fifty yards up Seventeenth Street we heard shots. At least five. We ran in that direction. I got a good look at the man who had fired the shots. He was light-skinned, with a fine-featured face with a mustache and beard starting to grow in, and was wearing a black hat. There was a gun in his left hand. He raised it to eye level, then lowered it, pulled down the brim of his hat and ran off. I said something about following him, but people talked me out of it. They said he would kill me."

"How did you recognize the assassin?" I asked. "How did you recall his appearance so clearly?"

"A few times after that I caught sight of him in the neighborhood. When I saw him I had no doubt. It was the same man. His name is Barreirito."

Tuesday, February 5. Last night Sister Lourdes and I got together with Heloisa, Aninha, Guaracy, Miguel LeMoal of the Pastoral Land Commission and Avelino Ganzer of the Central Labor Federation. We had learned through a telephone call from Itaituba about a meeting in that city at which it had been decided who in the south of Pará would die: Expedito, Raimundo Marques, someone else of the Rio Maria union whose name the person had forgotten, Father Hilário and me. They had gotten Expedito. Who would be next?

We talked about the need for a global strategy to counter the violence, to break the isolation of various groups and to unify the struggle. We needed to create Rio Maria Committees. They would be instruments of pressure, like the Chico Mendes Committees, so that these crimes would be exposed, those responsible would be punished and an end would be put to this spiral of assassinations. We were also concerned about the survival of the widows. Some state representatives were thinking about passing a law to get the government to support them.

Avelino took on the commitment to see that the labor federation would put one of their attorneys on these cases.

Meanwhile, the telephone never stopped ringing.

Thursday, February 7. Yesterday seven state police and ten soldiers of the Military Police entered the roadhouse Recreio Betânia, eighty-five kilometers from Rio Maria, where they arrested José Serafim Sales, known to everyone as Barreirito.

Yesterday I went to Conceição do Araguaia, where I took the opportunity to talk with the head of the regional office of the Pastoral Land Commission, Father Patrick O'Sullivan, along with other CPT staff members and union representatives, about the decisions taken by the group that met in Rio Maria. We discussed how to build on the decision made by the city council to set aside March 13 as the Day Against Violence. This would require mobilization and funds for telephone calls and transportation. We should invite human rights organizations from all over the country to participate. We also talked about supporting the decision of a group of lawyers to serve as assistants to the prosecution.

Guaracy proposed that we ask João Ripper, one of the photographers from Imagens da Terra, to help us design a poster to publicize the March 13 event.

Then we debated the issue of the continued death threats. Some people thought I should leave the area. I said I would discuss my safety only in conjunction with a discussion of the safety of the others.

"Would you suggest to the threatened farmers that they move?" I asked. "Where would they go? How would they live?"

I got a phone call from Father Henri des Roziers.

"If I can be of any help," he said, "I'll postpone my trip to Guatemala and spend three months or so in Rio Maria."

"Yes, Henri!" I immediately replied. "You'll be a great help!"

Saturday, February 9. Dona Isabel, a thin woman of nearly 60 who wears a white kerchief, was seated, bent over, and speaking in a soft thread of a voice.

"Every day we pray the rosary. Mother and I were praying and were not at all frightened by the gun shots."

I moved closer to hear her better.

"But then we got the news. I was so shocked. They had to take me to the hospital. My mother has stronger nerves. She didn't need to leave the house."

There was a long silence. Then Dona Isabel began reminiscing.

"We came from Teófilo Otoni in Minas Gerais. Father and Mother had eleven children, mostly boys. We moved first to Espírito Santo, where we lived for seven years. It was there that Expedito fell in love with Maria José. After that we went to Goiás. We lived in Porangatu and in São Miguel do Araguaia. The life of the poor is painful. Always pushed, driven like cattle. Rio Maria was the end of the journey."

Her face is full of sadness. It is as though she lost a son, rather than a brother. Sixteen years older than Expedito, she was like a second mother. Dona Isabel covered her face with her large peasant hands.

"Were you expecting this to happen, Dona Isabel?"

"Yes, the way things were going. I told him to be careful. One day I said, 'Brother, I'm afraid. Get out of that struggle.' He picked up a piece of paper. He was never without it, with his addiction to writing. Then he said that he would not get out of it. 'We're always dying, you know that, don't you, sister? Within the struggle or outside of it. I always have to be involved in the struggle. It's my destiny.' He was right. I was wrong. But it's so painful."

The silence is broken by her faster breathing. Her muscles tighten. She wipes away a tear.

"He was so patient," she murmured. "His weapon was poetry. He didn't even have a jackknife. And the rich people hired a gunman."

"Do you feel anger toward the man who killed your brother?" I asked.

"No, I have no anger. I feel only sorrow. So much sorrow."

The press people are still in the city. All the big papers have given generous space to our news. Marcelo Auler, from the *Jornal do Brasil*, published the most thorough article. This morning I talked with my friend Luís Maklouf, who works for the *Jornal da Tarde* in São Paulo.

Roberto, Carlos and Orlando came to the parish house looking tense. They feel the danger closing in. I invited them in and closed the door.

"Yesterday a journalist was in a bar," said Orlando. "He heard some ranchers saying that Roberto should die."

"Someone came looking for us," said Carlos. "He told us that these same men are going to stop Orlando from going back to Belém. They say that they're going to finish him off by tomorrow."

In spite of the heat Orlando was wearing a jacket. He took it off. It was soaked with sweat. It was then that I noticed that he had begun to carry a gun and was wearing the jacket to hide it. The federal government is still refusing to provide security.

After lunch we took Expedito's family to the cemetery. Besides visiting the grave of Expedito, we visited those of João Canuto, of his sons José and Paulo, of Brás and of Ronan. There are no identifying markers, because their families are poor.

19.

February 9 to March 4, 1991

Despite the atmosphere of fear and threat, people in Rio Maria begin to get organized to put an end to the violence.

Saturday, February 9. I was invited to a union meeting. The hall was full of farmers. At the main table were people who were under death threats — Orlando, Carlos, Roberto and Valdério.[1] They invited me to sit with them. Valdério was speaking.

"They'll never succeed in shutting down the union, unless they kill all the farmers. This is a class struggle. On one side the farmers, on the other the ranchers. We have to struggle to bring about a solution for our country."

Orlando was next with the microphone.

"I am enraged about the death of our comrade. What is the explanation for these assassinations? First of all, the authorities don't bring about agrarian reform; second, the Constitution discriminates against farmers. They want us to be slaves and a source of wealth for others. The murders happen because of a confrontation between a disorganized working class and an organized bourgeoisie. The best tribute that we can give to the dead is organization. Expedito remains alive if we continue his struggle. They call for violence. We call for justice. But justice is on their side! This society is still not ours!"

Applause. Carlos took the floor.

"We are meeting with our heads held high. The number of people here is larger than we had hoped. With the death of Expedito, they thought that they were going to wipe out our struggle. They didn't succeed. We have never seen a large landowner arrested. But we are going to show them that it doesn't do any good to kill one of us because the struggle always continues."

"The deaths in Rio Maria have a political aspect," said Roberto.

1. Valdério Pereira dos Santos is a former president of the Union of Rural Workers — tr.

"Because our struggle is not in the interest only of farmers. It is in the interest of the whole country. The bourgeoisie say that we want to grab the land. That's a lie. We want the land to be for everyone. We don't want the land to sell it, or to speculate on it, but to produce on it, to put food on tables. The union is not going to stop the struggle. We are not in favor of violence. We want peace. We organized this meeting as a challenge. All of you have to support this struggle. There is a list of those marked to die. So if someone knows about a gunman who intends to kill us, let us know."

He asked Antônio Vieira, president of the Teachers' Union, to speak.

"I want to say in the name of the union that this assembly was an act of heroism. This struggle belongs to all of us. When an act of such barbarism as this one happens, our wish is to get the gunman and identify him. We cannot forget, however, that there are those who hired him. Gunmen can only exist as long as there are people who pay them."

Later I talked on the phone with Frei Betto. He suggested that I go to São Paulo and to Rio de Janeiro for a meeting with the international press. João Ripper suggested the same. Cristiano, a Belgian journalist, advised me that the president of the Association of Foreign Journalists of Rio de Janeiro is interested in my going. I discussed this with the Pastoral Team and with Aninha of the Pastoral Land Commission. They were unanimous in saying that I should go.

After evening mass Vilma came into the parish house. She was tense and wanted to speak in private.

"You must take care of yourself. My daughter, Fátima, came home crying. She heard from the sister of a politician that you are the next to die."

"Did she say why?" I asked. "How did she know?"

Vilma didn't know. She would try to find out.

The telephone rang. It was Bel, my sister, apprehensive because of newspaper reports. In São Paulo they were saying that I would be one of the next to die.

After we hung up the phone rang again. It was Alda Maria, one of Carlos's sisters, a nun, calling from Mato Grosso.

"I saw the television and I got worried. I'm shocked about the death of Expedito. Tell Carlos that I'm praying for him. He must be uneasy."

There is no one else in the house. I am alone with my fears, doubts and fragility.

> Take down the hammock
> bind your heart with hope
> cut the brushwood, clear the field
> it's the time of fire
> it's the time of fire
>   fire
> temper with fire your brow
> temper with fire your lips

temper with fire your arms
and your feet

Take down the hammock
fire is hot and painful
uncrossable the clearing?
uncrossable the river?
unquenchable the blazing eyes

Sunday, February 10. A little before lunch I passed by the bus station. Some young girls with long skirts, blouses with sleeves down to the wrist, hair in enormous braids, were distributing flyers. Timidly a girl offered me one. In big print at the top was the title, "OPEN LETTER TO THE POPULATION." The letter, signed by the Youth Union of the Assembly of God, announced the growing risks of "moral and spiritual depravity." It announced that Carnival, "behind the masks, the follies, the samba schools, is a supernatural diabolical operation, a veritable demonic organization to destroy your life and that of thousands of people." It spoke of young people dominated by drugs, hundreds of separated couples, the death of spiritual life. It concluded with, "Donate your Carnival to Christ. Participate in a great Evangelical and spiritual crusade. Say no to Carnival. Say yes to Jesus."

Father Henri arrived with his shoulder bag and his good humor. We moved the dining table out to the veranda and turned the dining area into a room for him.

Monday, February 11. Carlos came into the parish house with Roberto. I invited them into the office. Roberto sat down beside the table. Carlos lay down on the bed and closed his eyes.

"I'm afraid," Roberto confessed. "I've never felt so afraid."

I told him that we had talked about the matter of security.

"I've already thought about leaving, because of schooling for my sons. I went to elementary school with the Orionite Fathers and I'd like for my sons to be able to study with them. But I don't really want to leave the city. What I would like to do is move to a different neighborhood. Passing through the area where João Canuto was shot is dangerous. Carlos should leave Vila Nova, too."

"Carlos, what do you think?" I asked.

He opened his eyes. "I don't want to move out and leave the others behind."

A friend who had had a visit from Expedito the night before he died came looking for me. Expedito told him that he had met with the police chief, who accused him of murders in Suaçuí. Expedito denied it, saying that he had never killed anyone or ordered anyone killed. Then the chief accused me. Expedito said that was not true, and, in fact, I was away on vacation. Still not satisfied, the chief went on to accuse Sister Lourdes. The friend concluded by saying, "Expedito believed that the next one to suffer an assassination attempt would be you."

It is almost midnight. In front of the parish house, there are about twenty-five young people of the Assembly of God singing religious hymns in their vigil against Carnival. From the side street the sound truck from the Big Boy Club is drowning them out.

We've just finished a meeting of the coordinating team of the Rio Maria Committee. Sebastião Vieira told us that Barreirito had been hanging around in front of his house.

A group of performing artists in Rio de Janeiro are preparing a manifesto of artists and intellectuals about the problem of Rio Maria.

The City Council is sending a document to the attorney general of the Republic, to the Federal Supreme Court and to the Ministry of Justice asking for action from the government in this region.

Ash Wednesday, February 13. Beginning of Lent.

Waters

How can I pour out my consciousness
into the River of Hope,
made and remade without pretense?
On that last night of agony
Fifteen leagues I rowed,
watched over by the moon,
pursued by the waters,
I drew from them my comfort;
from love my senselessness.
I buried in the past
That last night of agony.
When the rod is broken,
the fish will go free,
in the clearest waters.
In the River of Hope.

Dona Silvina brings me some curd cheese and stays to talk.

"In December I heard someone in the *Bate-Papo* Bar saying, 'Father Ricardo is marked to die. He and Expedito.' This week, when I found out about the death of Expedito, I got worried. They were condemning you and Father Pedro, saying that you were distributing weapons. Then just a little while ago I was at the marketplace and two women were talking. One was saying: 'I don't know why the newspapers are making such a fuss. Only one person died, and he was black and poor.' I let loose my tongue and said: 'Only one person died, but he was someone who defended many lives.'

They said that they didn't want to talk about it and that it was wrong to invade property."

Thursday, February 14. Father Henri is ready to go to work. Today we went together to the courthouse. The judge received us courteously and offered us coffee, water and tea. He told us about the conclusion of the inquests that investigated the deaths of Brás, Ronan, Paulo and José.

"There is too much talk about violence," he said. "People exaggerate. There is some violence. But it's from both sides."

I thought about the different kinds of violence. One is of the gunman, paid to kill. The other is of the farmer, who struggles for his life and defends himself from the bullets.

We had a good meeting with the prosecuting attorney. He seems to be a serious man who measures his words.

Today the lawyer and nun Suely Bellato arrived from São Paulo to help with the trials. She brought a copy of a letter directed to President Collor, signed by five United States senators and representatives,[2] writing about the assassination of Expedito and asking for protection for the lives of those still threatened.

Saturday, February 16. John Maier, Time-Life correspondent, traveled with us to Redenção for a meeting to organize the Day Against Violence and to create Rio Maria Committees throughout this region. Present were fifty-three representatives of seven municipal districts of the south of Pará. From Expedito's family came Dona Isabel, his daughter Antônia and his nephew João.

Dona Isabel, dressed in white, sat beside me and said: "Expedito was a prayerful man. Devout. He was a director of the Bible Circle and he prepared children for first communion. Ever since he was a boy he was concerned about justice."

Dona Isabel gave testimony in the plenary session.

"We see these events that seem to have no end. Each day the sorrows are increased. I am very nervous about seeing Rio Maria with so many widows. Women without husbands, children without fathers. My brother struggled for better days. He knew that he could be the victim of tragic violence. He said that if he died, it would be for the people of Rio Maria. He told me, 'The struggle must continue. There is no solution without struggle.' On Saturday he came home from Marabá. That afternoon he said that he was going out. Maria José asked him, 'Aren't you going to have supper?' He said that he was going to the union office to work on some papers because on the next day there would be a meeting. He went out to a neighbor's house to watch the news. Then he went to the union office.

2. The letter was dated February 12, 1991. Those who signed were Alan Cranston, Edward M. Kennedy, Barbara A. Mikulski, Mark O. Hatfield and Tom Harkin.

He did not stay long. He came back, walking up Tenth Avenue, and turned down Seventeenth Street. The gunman was waiting. His oldest daughter came down the path crying, 'Mother, they killed my father!' They wanted to shut the mouth of an honorable citizen."

Dona Isabel went back to her seat. Her niece Antônia got up to speak.

"He didn't talk about the threats at home. We found out through other people. Even with a pain in his stomach, he went to the union office without having supper. I was at a neighbor's house watching television when the news came. Mother had the youngest in her arms. She left the child on the bed and came running."

Carlos spoke next. "I was practically staying away from the union office because of the threats. That week we had the feeling that something was going to happen. There was a stranger, acting curious, spying. On Friday Expedito was called to the police station. I was worried. Roberto was out of town. Father Ricardo had not yet returned."

The attorneys Jorge Farias, Suely Bellato and Father Henri gave information regarding the police inquests and the judicial aspects.

During the recess I heard Sebastião Vieira, president of the City Council, saying, "The Council decided to do a careful examination of the accounts of the city government between 1986 and 1988. The Finance Commission, of which I was chair, discovered fraud. I put in a requisition for an outside audit. When the auditors came the telephone rang. One of them, Joel, answered and received a death threat. A few moments later, former Mayor Laranjeira passed by in his Gol in front of the council chamber. He was driving very slowly, observing. Another phone call. I answered and identified myself. He said, 'What are these persecutions against Laranjeira?' I answered that I knew nothing about persecutions. There was information about the audit. He said, 'You'd better be careful because you're going to die. You're persecuting me. Everyone who persecutes me dies. You know that.' Then he hung up. I called the judge to say that we were getting ready to register a complaint with the police. Officer Miranda received the complaints and said that he would pass them on to the judge. The audit turned up a discrepancy of 340,000,000 cruzeiros, according to the currency values of December 31, 1990 (US $2,129,729). The action to recover the stolen funds will begin next Monday."

More people gathered around as Sebastião continued speaking. "One time in 1984 or 1985, Laranjeira walked into City Hall, put his hand in his bag and said that he would cut me down with lead. I reported this to the police. There were two witnesses, Expedito and Mário Antônio. He was wild because I was reporting him for having used the machinery of the city government for his own ends."

During the meeting we discussed the Day Against Violence and made decisions about invitations, organizing, housing, food, transportation and security. Among those to be invited were victims of the violence: widows, orphans, witnesses, and people who have been shot or beaten. They would have the opportunity to speak to the government authorities who would be present.

Wednesday, February 20. There are various messages in the telephone notebook, some from the press, others from friends who are doing the organizing. There was also a call from London. It was Francisco from Amnesty International. This organization is getting ready to put out an urgent action asking for the investigation of the deaths, punishment of those responsible and protection of the lives of Raimundo Marques, Carlos Cabral, Roberto Neto, Valdério Pereira dos Santos, Orlando Canuto and me. Congressman Valdir Ganzer is preparing a formal petition for the plenary session of Congress to request the formation of a Commission of Federal Congressmen to participate in the demonstration on March 13 in Rio Maria.

Thursday, February 21. There was a police investigation of the Nazaré Ranch, where Éder Mauro and his team arrested the manager, Francisco de Assis Ferreira, known as Grilo, and confiscated a veritable arsenal. The rancher, Jerônimo Alves de Amorim, escaped arrest because he was not there. Barreirito, in his deposition, said that he killed Expedito for 200,000 cruzeiros (US $833.33). He accused Jerônimo of having ordered the death and Grilo as having served as the intermediary. The police confiscated a check register in which Expedito's name was written in Grilo's handwriting. The value of the check was exactly 30,000 cruzeiros (US $125), which corresponds to the first payment.

Cristina Pereira called to say that they had already collected more than two hundred signatures for the Manifesto.

At the next meeting of the diocesan council we're going to discuss the possibility of strengthening the work of the Rio Maria Committee by hiring Juvenila and André as staff persons. They could be funded through the diocesan citizenship formation project.

Sebastião Vieira came to see me. He said, "City Councilor Argemiro talked with the brother of Barreirito. He said that Barreirito was hired by Jerônimo at the Nazaré Ranch. There was a barbecue at which Laranjeira was present. After the barbecue Jerônimo asked how much the gunman wanted. They agreed on 200,000, with 30,000 in advance."

There have been hundreds of letters from Brazil and several other countries, from individuals and organizations, protesting the violence and expressing solidarity with our struggle.

Saturday, March 2. I had a meeting with three correspondents from the foreign press and eight from the national press in São Paulo at the headquarters of the newspaper union. I also taped an interview with Jô Soares. During the interview a fax came in from the movie actress Ana Carolina. It was a copy of the Manifesto of the artists and intellectuals. Jô read the text, looked at the enormous list of signers and said that he would sign as well. In Rio de Janeiro there was a meeting with twenty-seven foreign correspondents at the Rio Palace Hotel. Some of the national press were there, along with several friends.

Tuesday, March 4. This afternoon we had a meeting of the coordinating group of the Rio Maria Committee to discuss the thirteenth. We already received confirmation of the presence of Paulo Betti, Bishop Augusto (national president of the Pastoral Land Commission), Lula, Senators Suplicy and Gabriel, various federal and state deputies and the president of CONTAG, Aloísio Carneiro.

Carlos and Roberto were the last ones to leave. We said good-bye and I went back into my office. The phone hadn't been working right. We couldn't call out, but could receive incoming calls. That always seems to happen whenever something important is going on.

I heard voices outside. One sounded like Roberto. He had left less then twenty minutes earlier. I went out to see what was wrong. He was coming back with Carlos, who was limping.

"What happened, Roberto?"

"We were going up the street by the cemetery. The wall around it has some gaps. From one of those holes someone took aim at us. He fired two shots over our heads, and the third one got Carlos in the leg."

Carlos silently showed me the two holes in his jeans. The bullet had passed through his leg and gone back out.

It was in front of that same cemetery that they had assassinated Carlos's father-in-law, João Canuto.

We had to get immediate medical attention and security measures. For the first, we went looking for Doctor Haroldo. But where could we get security? The judge, the police chief and the mayor were all out of town. Who could guarantee that these gunmen would not try again? The telephone rang. I answered. It was Ricardo Soca, correspondent for the Spanish newspaper *El País*, calling from Rio de Janeiro. I asked him to give information to other journalists and to people at the Pastoral Land Commission. The telephone was no longer silent. Our isolation was broken. Friends were calling, sharing solidarity, denouncing the violence.

Epilogue

The Devil Creates the Pot, God the Lid

The tremulous flame of the oil wick lit the inside of the small hut, projecting wavering shadows on the rough walls. I went to the window and spent a long time looking at the star-filled sky. Fireflies were slicing the air in their irregular flight, as though trying with their small light to compete with the stars. Seu Zé pulled up the rough wooden stool, sat down, picked up a corn husk and began pulling off the end of a wad of tobacco. The peasant farmer's fingers looked like roots of a tree. I stood with my back to the window and watched him. At times the light of the wick illumined his face, leaving one side in darkness. When the light became weaker, he would almost disappear into the shadows. I was thinking of paintings by Rembrandt with their light and shadows, or when the light would distort the image, the expressionist *Ecce Homo* of Georges Rouault. Christ crowned with thorns and humiliated. Face, hands and feet, calloused and suffering. A pure expression of pain in the wrinkles that divided his body into dozens of tiny triangles, squares and rectangles.

"Father Ricardo," said Seu Zé. "We are giving a Bible course in the base community. The people like it a lot. We take the word of God and compare it to life. God is animating the path of the people in history. It's beautiful."

His eyes are sparkling. A crucified Christ? No. The Christ of Van Dyck, resurrected, bathed in light. Or the Lord at Emmaus by Velazquez. I feel the urge to grab a canvas and water colors. It's been a long while since I've had time to work with paint and paper.

"So we talk," he continued. "We explain that the church could be like the cashew—with the seed separate from the fruit,[1] staying on the outside. A church that thinks that the world is only sin and that prefers to keep its distance. It could also be like an avocado, with the pit inside the fruit, but without being a part of it, considering itself pure, like oil in water. But that doesn't work either. It has to be like the seed of an orange, that is spread throughout the fruit, that enters into each pulpy segment. So when we are

---

1. The cashew nut, which is plentiful in Northern Brazil, grows *outside* of the cashew fruit—tr.

persecuted, the church gives help, not betrayal. It understands. It is light, salt and leaven."

The word of God should break into this world to bring hope, to give new life, to resurrect dreams and to bring about better times. Seu Zé lives in these woods, far from the city, from medical care, from schools. The arrival of the priest is a big event. I come here poor, without much wisdom, to participate in the faith, and I end up drinking from this well of living water. His eyes speak of hope.

As I am looking at Seu Zé, I also think of Helena, leader of three base communities, an untiring evangelizer. She walks eight kilometers to give leadership to the Três Reis community or to Maria de Nazaré, without neglecting her work of coordinating the Cristo Redentor community, where she lives. She travels by narrow forest trails, on dark nights, lighting her way with an old lantern. Her rubber thong sandals pass through so much mud and pick up so much dust on behalf of the Kingdom of God. How small I feel! We priests have a lot to learn from the witness of these people.

Seu Zé hands me an old book, worn and yellowed. I leaf through it. I see that he has used it a lot, underlining the most important words and making little annotations in any spaces he could find. His twisted hand-writing and spelling errors show that he has had very little schooling. It was from this book that he took the analogy of the three fruits to express his understanding of the role of the church. He brought the book with him from the diocese of Governador Valadares in the state of Minas Gerais. Seu Zé is a migrant, as are the majority of the people of this parish.

My God, thirty-two million Brazilians live in a state of absolute poverty. Ten million farmers travel across this country without land or work. How long will this situation continue? Helena, Seu Zé and all the adults of this region came from other cities or states. New Abrahams and Sarahs, driven by need, looking for land, peace, prosperity and tranquility in a country with so much land that is idle and fit for cultivation. Some will find what they are looking for, while others continue to face enormous difficulties. Forced labor, beatings and murder are part of the daily lives of these people.

What should be the role of the church in this world where there are angels but also demons? Where heaven and hell do battle with each other? Where one cannot preach to the clouds and where the moments of trans-figuration are rare? There is a permanent temptation to stay on top of the hill, to wish, as did Peter (Luke 9:37-43), to build tabernacles and not to come down into the valley of contradictions and conflicts. Jesus and the apostles did come back down, however, and immediately faced the desperate request of a man who wanted help for his only son. The child would cry out, violently convulsing and foaming at the mouth. Jesus healed the child and everyone was amazed.

Peter (Matthew 16:13-28) did not want Jesus to go to Jerusalem, and

Jesus, who had just been praising him, spoke harshly: "Get out of my sight, you Satan."

There are temptations to flee from Jerusalem, from the valleys and the plains, to let one's feet leave the ground and to look only upward. The church constantly needs to hear the question of the angels:

So why are you looking up at the sky? This Jesus who has been taken from you will return, just as you saw him go up into the heavens.

It is so much simpler to forget the tensions, the conflicts, and to seek only private, individual answers. It is so much simpler to gaze upward and to be dazzled by the light of one's own desires. But God stirs us and calls us to put our feet on this earth. He sends those who summon us and shake our consciences and the structures of the church.

The entries in this book end on March 4, 1991, with the shooting of Carlos Cabral, current president of the union, one month after the murder of Expedito. Carlos survived. Others were not so fortunate. Between 1980 and 1992 at least 180 rural workers were killed in our diocese. Because of these deaths, we have made a great deal of effort to sensitize public opinion in Brazil regarding social injustice and murder for hire. As a result the number of deaths of peasant farmers in our diocese has decreased. In 1985 fifty-four were killed. In 1991 there were six murders and twelve disappearances. In 1992 the number fell to four murders and one disappearance. The difference is impressive, but the killings are still tragic. Ten percent of all deaths of rural workers in this country in 1992 were related to land conflicts or flight from forced labor.

How can this serious problem be resolved? We need to have a new form of land use. We cannot continue to coexist with the terrible reality that some people have properties the size of nations, while many others live as beggars. *Veja*, one of the magazines with the largest weekly distribution in Brazil, published a report on July 7, 1993, about the lords of the lands and the forests:

The big landowners in Brazil have lands the size of countries, but they don't raise livestock, they don't plant crops, and sometimes they cheat on their taxes.

The article did not mention Mr. Daniel Ludwig, the late North American billionaire, who had holdings of millions of acres, or of Volkswagen, Nixdorf and other companies, who sold their ranches in recent years. They do, however, cite some cases, such as that of Pedro Dotto, who had over four million acres, an area comparable to El Salvador, and Mário Jorge Moraes, with two and a half million acres, the size of Jamaica. His property is valued at 1.6 billion dollars, but he employs only three hundred families and owes forty thousand dollars in property taxes. The article presented other cases, like that of Malih Eumaoula, with one million acres, almost half the size of Lebanon, his country of origin. There is also Leônidas Meirelles de Queiroz, with nearly two million acres, an area larger than Puerto Rico.

It is certain that this concentration of land is not God's plan. Pope John Paul II himself, passing through Brazil, said that "all private property carries a social mortgage." There is a series of warnings, formulated by prophets since the Hebrew scriptures, against the iniquity of those who use land as an instrument of oppression.

> Woe to you who join house to house, who connect field with field, till no room remains, and you are left to dwell alone in the midst of the land! (Isaiah 5:8).

In 1980 the National Conference of Brazilian Bishops published a document called "The Church and Land Problems." It is a document that analyzes the question of landed property and the grave consequences of flagrant injustice. It demonstrates the reality of the facts, presents the doctrinal foundation and concludes with "Our Pastoral Commitment." Land is a subject that unites the church in Brazil. The inequality and the violence is of such magnitude that the bishops, whatever their usual positions as conservatives or progressives, usually take a position in favor of agrarian reform.

Shortly after the assassination of Expedito, people from several towns in the south of Pará and from other parts of the country gathered to reflect on the problem of violence. Expedito's death drew a great deal of attention in the national press after articles were published in magazines and newspapers in other countries—in the United States, *Time* (March 4, 1991), *Newsweek* (March 4, 1991) and *The Nation* (April 1, 1991); in France, *Le Monde Diplomatique* (March, 1991), *Le Nouvel Observateur* (March 14-20, 1991), *Témoignage Crétien* (March 9, 1991); in Spain, *El Independiente* (March 5, 1991); in Germany, *Deutsches Allgemeines Sonntagsblatt* (March 15, 1991); and others. The nation was waking up to the drama in the rural areas, partly because the international press was beginning to speak up.

We needed to do something about the crimes that represent attempts to stifle the free expression of ideas and of political and union organization. The case of Expedito is not the only one. According to the document "Conflicts in the Countryside, Brazil, 1992,"[2] published by the Pastoral Land Commission:

> From January 1, 1964, to December 31, 1992, there were registered 1,730 assassinations of rural workers, Indians, lawyers, religious sisters, priests and other professionals linked to the rural poor people's

2. This is the most recently published annual report of the Pastoral Land Commission—tr.

movement. In the twenty-nine cases that were tried, fifty-three victims were involved. So the legal system passed judgment on only 2.8 percent of the known murders (according to the Department of Documentation of the Pastoral Land Commission). In the majority of the cases brought to trial, pressure from national and international public opinion was needed to make the trials happen. Almost one hundred of the victims were leaders of rural unions.

Rio Maria has become a symbol of this growing and selective violence. This was why we created the Rio Maria Committees, which quickly spread through Brazil and even to other countries. We needed to bring strong pressure on the Brazilian government, because that is the only way that we will be able to have peace and democracy and to put an end to this violence with impunity. We also needed to work through the judicial system. Although it is not possible to investigate all the crimes, we have a team of competent and known attorneys from various cities who have offered to work on the most pressing ones. Father Henri des Roziers, a sixty three-year-old Dominican friar and attorney, is coordinating this group.

On June 30, 1993, the trial for the murder of Expedito was to have taken place in Rio Maria. For the first time in the south of the state of Pará we were going to have a trial for a crime by a rancher against a peasant farmer. Three days before, however, lawyers for the defense entered a motion, alleging that there could not be an impartial trial in Rio Maria. They accused the church, without offering proof, of creating constraints for the jurors, and they asked for a change of venue to Xinguara, twenty-seven kilometers away. In reality there were other reasons for their motion. The rancher accused of ordering Expedito's death, Jerônimo Alves de Amorim, wanted the trial postponed. Also, since one of his properties is in Xinguara, many of the ranchers there are friendly toward him, as is the mayor, who is also suspected of being involved in the same crime. It is possible that Amorim is counting on the jurors' fear for their own lives. Guns are an especially strong means of persuasion in Xinguara, which has the highest rate of murders of farmers in the whole country.

The Court of Justice of the State Capital met two days before the trial and decided to move it ahead and to change the location. They made that decision without considering the fact that the judge of Rio Maria, the assistant judge and the prosecuting attorney were all opposed to the motion of the defense. They also did not consider the fact that the local judge had already spent municipal funds to paint and renovate the place where the trial would be held. They did not consider the fact that five hundred Military Police had been requested and that one hundred sixty were already in the city, which involved great expenditures for transportation, food, housing and daily wages. They did not consider that hundreds of representatives of national and international human rights organizations, journalists and members of embassies had made reservations in hotels, some with advance payment, that they had purchased their airline or bus tickets, and that some were already here. They did not consider that the judicial system already has a bad reputation and that this action would add to it.

Sometimes I feel embarrassed when someone marvels at our "courage" and "readiness to face difficulties." We have not come here out of heroism or sacrifice. We have experienced pleasure in learning, teaching, sharing dreams, traveling through the forest, talking, celebrating, seeing a people who are constructing their history in spite of so much pain and sorrow. As Christians, we know that God will have the last word, not the lords of the world, of weapons, of land, of capital. People here have a saying: The devil creates the pot, God the lid!

In Isaiah 55:10-11 God reminds us that the rain does not return to heaven without having watered and nourished the earth. "So shall be the word that goes forth from my mouth; it shall not return without having done my will."

Indeed, as the biblical writer said, when the sun punishes the earth, the fire devours the forests and pastures, a black carpet covers the countryside, everything appears to have ended. After the first rain, however, the green bursts forth from this ground and life explodes in the soil . . .

Here also God pours down the rain of his Word!

—RICARDO REZENDE
Feast of Saints Peter and Paul, 1993